COMMON YET UNCOMMON

Celebrating 35 Years of
Penguin Random House India

COMMON YET UNCOMMON

14
Memorable
Stories from
Daily Life

SUDHA MURTY

PENGUIN BOOKS
An imprint of Penguin Random House

PENGUIN BOOKS

USA | Canada | UK | Ireland | Australia
New Zealand | India | South Africa | China | Singapore

Penguin Books is part of the Penguin Random House group of companies
whose addresses can be found at global.penguinrandomhouse.com

Published by Penguin Random House India Pvt. Ltd
4th Floor, Capital Tower 1, MG Road,
Gurugram 122 002, Haryana, India

First published in Penguin Books by Penguin Random House India 2023

Copyright © Sudha Murty 2023

All rights reserved

10 9 8 7 6 5 4 3 2 1

ISBN 9780143464617

Typeset in Sabon by Manipal Technologies Limited, Manipal
Printed at Thomson Press India Ltd, New Delhi

www.penguin.co.in

To Akshata and Rohan,
born between the land of rivers
Tungabhadra and Krishna.

Contents

Contents

Preface

The river Tungabhadra divides Karnataka into two parts—North and South. The northern part of Karnataka has its peculiar history. It was the capital seat of the state for a thousand years before it was ruled by the Kadambas, Chalukyas, Rashtrakutas, the glorious Vijayanagar emperors and the Shi'ite Adil Shahis, followed by the Sunni Mughals, the warrior Marathas and finally the British colonizers. Different rulers followed different cultures, food habits and languages. This impacted the people of the region. There was an amalgamation of cultures, languages and food habits. Even a different dialect was born out of it, which stands apart from its counterparts. The people here use a mixture of Persian, Arabic and Marathi words. Their food habits are also very different. You can see a variety of North and South Karnataka dishes. People from the North use a special *kala* masala packed with forty-two spices. And every dish is prepared in various ways. For example, the simple poli has many spins. There is peanut poli, sesame poli, roasted gram poli, besan poli and so on. The chutneys are made of ridge gourd, flaxseeds, pumpkin, brinjal, amla, mango, etc. This history makes its presence felt in the region's wedding customs as well as other rituals, which are usually short and not ostentatious. By and large, the people here are open-minded and outspoken, much like the flat and open land that Mother Nature has bestowed on them.

I am sure such diversity exists in every Indian state. For instance, the Maharashtrians of Pune are very different from those in Nagpur. Similarly, North Goans are different from their Southern counterparts. No wonder it's said for every 150 kilometres that you travel in our country, you will see a change in food habits and dressing styles. In a way, Mother India is not one country but has many nations within her. She represents a continent.

I have chosen Karnataka as the setting for this book since it is my homeland. I grew up in a middle-class family in North Karnataka and am well-versed with the customs of its community, though I have immensely changed with time. In the stories of this book, I portray a bunch of uncommon personalities from this land who were a part of my growing-up years. I have learnt something from each of them. These people were not famous—neither did they get any recognition in society, nor did they crave it. Yet, each one is unique. Apart from lacking fame, these personalities were not rich or qualified. Yet, I have found some magnanimity in them. These people have a transparent mind and are outspoken. They are not polished, neither in their speech nor in their appearance. The crude veneer is no testimony to their unparalleled love and affection. They may not be business-minded, but their society is simple, straightforward and helpful. As the English language cannot express the complexities of any Indian dialect, I might not be able to do justice to the parlance of my home town, but I hope I can give you a glimpse of a few unembellished characters from North Karnataka.

In our region, no one likes to be addressed by their actual names. They always use pet names, or keep the names short. Hence, you can find different characters with shortened names such as Pari, Palya and Raghu. They are substitutes for Parimala, Prahlad and Raghavendra, respectively. I appear as Nalini—fondly called Nali by several—in these stories, peeping in and out of every chapter, sometimes as a young girl, sometimes as a young adult and sometimes as a married woman. Each character in these stories is a pearl. I am just the thread that weaves into this necklace, which I owe to my people and my land.

I want to thank my young and bright editor Milee Ashwarya for bringing out this book, and Gaurav Shrinagesh for his kind support—both from Penguin Random House India.

1

Bundle Bindu

Bindu Madhav Patil was a young man no less handsome than a film star. He had nice sharp features, was well-built and had a crown of silky jet-black hair. Above all, he had a pleasant smile and great confidence.

He would seldom invite anyone home. He visited people most of the time. But once, I had to visit him at his home for some work that my grandmother had given me.

I did not know his address and was hesitant to ask him because, in our city, there are no mains and crosses for any location.

The addresses shared by the people there are rather descriptive. Like, if I have to ask for the address to our home, Dr Kulkarni's house, I would have to trace his family history first. It would go something like this: 'The doctor is a good man. He has a white dog, who always sleeps near the gate, and when a stranger comes, he becomes friendly and welcomes them. However, the dog gets upset with its people. The doctor has only one son and has married a Punjabi girl.'

Then it would be easy for the person, to whom I would have asked this address, to recollect the directions to the home. It would go something like this: '. . . Oh, that Dr Kulkarni? It is very easy—take a left, then first right and first left. Left side, third house.'

I wondered, with such elaborate narration, how could I ever find Bindu's house?

But Bindu said, 'Nali, it is so simple. Take a bus to Netaji Nagar. Get off at the last stop. Take ten steps ahead. There you have a big hoarding of Keerti Stores. The store owner is a close friend of mine—you just mention my name and he will accompany you and drop you to my house.'

I was surprised by these directions. 'Are you sure?' I asked.

'Nali, don't ask too many questions. You are a high school student. This is the address I give to everyone, and they reach my home without a problem.'

Hesitantly, I took the Netaji Nagar bus. I got off at the last stop and as per his directions, I walked ten steps ahead. There was nothing there. I walked a hundred steps but couldn't see anything. I continued to walk another two hundred steps and yet couldn't see any hoarding of Keerti Stores. Helplessly, I asked a passerby on the road, 'Where is Keerti Stores?'

The man said, 'You have come too far. You should have gotten down one stop before the last stop.'

'What should I do now?'

In a detached tone, he said, 'Walk back the way you have come.'

And I did just that. Soon enough, I saw a small cardboard hoarding hanging on an electric pole. On it, 'Keerti Stores' was written in chalk. Bindu's 'big hoarding' was nowhere in sight.

A sleepy shopkeeper was sitting on a stool. The store had chocolates, peppermints and cool drinks. When he saw me, he woke up and showed enthusiasm. There were no customers in sight. With a broad smile, he said, 'Please come. What would you like to buy?'

'I want to go to Bindu Patil's house . . .'

'I am not selling that item here,' he said, upset.

'Bindu told me to ask you for directions.'

'He says a hundred things. Not all are true. Tomorrow if he says that I will become the chief minister, will I become one?'

The owner of the shop seemed to take out his frustration on me. I kept quiet.

Then, he cooled down. This is typical of North Karnataka's people. First, we get upset, and then we help. Just like a jackfruit—thorny on the outside and sweet on the inside. He asked, 'Which Bindu Patil's house do you want to go to?'

I didn't know how to answer but with great difficulty, I said, 'He is handsome, like a film star.'

'This locality does not have any film stars' residences. For that, you have to go to Bangalore or Bombay. Where does he work? What does he do?'

'I don't know.' Despite knowing him for a long time, I had no clue about his professional endeavours.

'He is unemployed then?' The shop owner was getting frustrated since I was unable to provide him with details. 'There are many Bindu Patils in this area—there is an Insurance Bindu, a Drunkard Bindu and Bindu, the Teacher.'

Suddenly I remembered something. 'His wife, Saraswati, is a teacher.'

'Oh, you should have said that first. Then I wouldn't have spoken so much. You want to go to Bundle Bindu's house. Anyway, now I will give you the directions.'

He leaned forward from his place behind the row of jars and stretching out his hand as much as he could, he pointed the route for my next journey.

'Take a right turn here, then a fourth left turn and the sixth house on the left side in pink colour is Bundle Bindu's,' he said.

I thanked him and followed his directions till I reached my destination. Almost immediately, I got a hint as to why Bindu was called Bundle Bindu.

When I saw the house, I saw two name plates on each side of the main gate—Bindu Madhav Patil on one side and 'Satyadhama' on the other.

I wondered, what a contrast that *Satyadhama* and Bundle Bindu were at the same place.

In Bindu's dictionary, the word 'no' does not exist. He did not get upset when people insulted him. No matter what work you told him to do, he would never say no. But most of the time, he wouldn't do it either. I hardly saw him tell the truth without exaggeration. Perhaps that was the reason he got the prefix 'Bundle'—the one who wraps people in his talk.

Many times, my grandmother would scold him, 'Bindya, to explain one incident, you will add a hundred scenes to it. If I ask you to do any work, you will never complete it. You are unpredictable. I remember when your mother was pregnant with you, you didn't come for nine months and nine days. Instead, you came on a day when no one was expecting you.'

Nobody knew about his education, including his wife, Saraswati.

Before his marriage, Bindu's father had told Saraswati's father, 'My son has started a business, which he says is doing well. He has a degree as well.'

Bindu's and Saraswati's fathers were good friends. The bride's father saw the board of Raghava Enterprises in front of the house—*business must indeed be doing well.* Also, the groom looked smart and spoke good English.

Saraswati agreed and the wedding took place. The elders of her family were so simple that the 'Raghava Enterprise' board was enough for them to believe in Bindu's booming business. They could have never imagined that one could name their business after a God and still not work.

Saraswati, an ordinary-looking girl, was an introvert by nature. After her marriage, she continued to work as a schoolteacher and looked after the family. She didn't question her husband. Bindu would tell her a hundred stories. In the end, he would say, 'This is a dull season for my business. Loan me two hundred rupees. I will return it next month.'

At first, Saraswati gave him the money but soon realized that the dull season was a frequent visitor—Bindu would never return the money. So, she began giving him only fifty rupees. Yet, to my knowledge, I had never heard of the couple fighting, maybe because Saraswati didn't expect anything from him. Soon, they became a small family of three after they had their child.

My grandfather would say, 'Everybody's veins have blood, but in Bindu's veins, exaggeration flows.'

If you listen to Bindu's stories, they are funny.

Recently, he had come to our home and was talking to my aunts.

'I wrote a letter to Obama that he should visit Hubli and its neighbouring areas,' he said. 'After all, America is only two hundred years old. Our region is two thousand years old,' Bindu said.

'Is it?' my aunt asked him, despite knowing that it wasn't true, but the innocent children believed it.

'Of course. I also explained to him the history of Karnataka. He should see Hampi where gold and diamonds were sold on the streets without fear during the Vijayanagar Empire. He should come with his family. He should also see Lakkundi and listen to the story of Attimabbe.'

'Bindu, why will he learn about Attimabbe?' I asked.

The question was enough to upset him. 'Nali, you don't know the value of history? If you don't know of Attimabbe, it is a disgrace.'

He forgot about Obama and began to speak about Attimabbe, the widow queen from the tenth century. As I had heard the story many times from him, I tried to stop him. 'I know the history of Attimabbe,' I said.

'You may know it, Nali, but Obama doesn't.'

He scolded me for the next five minutes, by the end of which he had forgotten the origin of the conversation.

'What was I talking about before?'

'Obama.'

'Now, I want to write to Trump. He has been strict about H-1B visas. If we did the same in India, no foreigner would come to our country and enjoy our heritage, food and culture. What a loss!'

He had now transformed into an immigration officer.

'Did Obama reply?'

'Of course. He is tired after working for eight years and requires rest. Next time, he will bring his family, including his children when they have a holiday. He also said I should come to America and explain the history of Karnataka. His letter upset me.'

'Did it really?' I asked, to tease him.

'Yes. Look at our country. Look at our history. What wonderful dynasties we had in Karnataka and the north of the country.' Again, Bindu took off on another track. He knew his history very well and, of course, had a knack for exaggerating.

For us children, he was our honorary history teacher, often calling us to different places—such as under the shade of a banyan tree—to teach us the subject in his style. We were tired of the history teachers at our school. History was always the last period, and the teacher would rattle off a bunch of names and dates. 'Children, listen to me—1336 was when the Vijayanagar Empire was established; 1680—Shivaji's death; 1776—American War of Independence.' Often, she would tell me to continue the lesson, because she had some work in the teacher's room. As she exited, I became the teacher and would say, 'We have Kadambas, Chalukyas, Rashtrakutas . . .' Whatever knowledge I had was because of Bindu's lessons. But nobody would listen to me, and all the students would run away to the playground. Only Bindu could breathe life in such dry history.

Bindu's father owned a farm, where they grew fruits. They also had a stepwell. During summer, Bindu would take all of us friends and cousins to bathe there. His history sessions would follow in the garden below the tamarind tree. It was during these sessions that I learnt about the entire history of Karnataka, and about the men and women who fought for our country's freedom. I learnt of 'Jhansi ki Rani' Lakshmi Bai, Tatya Tope, Mumtaz Mahal and Akbar the Great. Then he would make us compete through a test. The winners would get fruits from his garden. By the time we reached home, it would be late. We were scolded by everyone, especially my grandmother. 'That Bindya does not have any job and all of you go sit in his garden and eat all the fruits. The poor chap, his father, works so hard to maintain the garden.'

But we didn't stop.

On full moon nights, all of us friends, guided by Bindu, would gather for a potluck dinner on the terrace of someone's home. I still recollect the cool, quiet moonlight shining on the floor and handsome Bindu giving us history lessons—narrations on Chhattrapati Shivaji and how he killed Afzal Khan, or the way Chetak died at Haldighati, or how Rana Pratap died or on Rani Karnavati who sent a rakhi to Humayun, or on Krishna Deva Raya winning all the wars he fought and Dussehra festivities in the Vijayanagara Empire or on the *swayamvar* of Samyukta and her abduction by Prithviraj. His words would hypnotize us—we would lose ourselves in these imaginary stories.

Once, we sobbed after he had described the emperor Rama Raya, the son-in-law of Krishna Deva Raya and commander-in-chief of the Vijayanagar Army. Then he said, 'Because the son-in-law never earned the kingdom with hard work, he never valued it. We lost our freedom forever.'

My cousin Rohini got up, and said, 'I am not going to marry anyone named Rama.'

Many years later, my uncle brought a marriage proposal of a man for Rohini, but she refused to marry him because his name was Ram.

My grandfather, a history teacher, had observed how enchanted we were by Bindu's words. He intervened once, saying, 'Don't get carried away by Bindu's words. He knows the art of storytelling. A king could lose his empire for many reasons, such as internal tensions, laziness stemming from excessive wealth . . . even a good partnership with the Adil Shahis, was one of the reasons for defeat, or maybe the opposing side had better horses and weapons.'

We found his explanation to be lifeless. We preferred to believe Bindu despite all the holes and gaps in his stories.

His habit of exaggeration made people avoid him on certain occasions. For instance, Bindu was never called for any wedding negotiations. He would blow things out of proportion for both parties. To the boy's side, he would say, 'Don't worry, it will definitely be a three-day wedding. I promise you that on behalf of the girl's father.' To the girl's side, he would say, 'On behalf of the boy's father, I promise they will share half the expenses.'

As his family was small and did not have financial difficulties, he didn't know what wedding expenses in India truly meant.

While he was avoided on some occasions, he would be demanded on others. People travelling to the north for pilgrimage would ask for Bindu as he had a good command of Hindi. God alone knows where he learnt the language. He claimed to have learnt it from the movies.

One day, I met him when he had just returned from Kashi. He said, 'Travelling by train has become really dangerous.'

'What happened?' I asked.

'I went with the Desai family to Kashi. There was a full bogey of friends and relatives. But at some station in Uttar

Pradesh (UP), a gang of dacoits arrived on horses, got into the compartments, pulled the train to a stop and asked for gold and money.'

'Did you lose anything?'

'No, I always keep my money in the form of a traveller's cheque. But Leela Desai lost her *mangalasutra*. By the time the police arrived, the dacoits had run away.'

'What happened then?'

'I told the guards that this would never happen in Karnataka. I called the guard to instil fear in those dacoits.'

I really don't believe what he says. Who will listen to his Kannada in UP? But maybe there was an element of truth.

That evening, I went to Leela's house. I asked, 'How was your Kashi trip?'

'It was good except . . .'

'What?'

'There was a lot of rush in Kashi.'

'Did you lose anything?' I prodded her.

'Not really, just four old saris. I gave them to my husband to hold for me on the ghat. Somebody ran off with the bag when he was distracted. As usual, he was inefficient.'

She took a dig at her husband.

'I heard that there are train robberies in UP. Is that true?'

'Yes, people say so and I have seen it in the movies.'

I couldn't control myself any longer. I had to know. 'I heard you lost your mangalasutra?'

Casually, she said, 'Yes. I knew that I shouldn't carry my gold mangalasutra, so I bought a silver one for three hundred rupees. Somewhere near the station, it was very warm, so I opened the window shutter. Some petty thief pulled my mangalasutra and went away. But that's okay. I was prepared for such an incident. I feel bad for the thief. He won't get anything for it.'

'Didn't some dacoits come and make off with your mangalasutra?'

'Who told you that?'

'Bindu.'

'Nali, you don't have a brain. You are grown up now. How can you believe what he says? His name says it all.'

The other day (after several years), Bindu was sitting and writing something. I had never seen him write before, only talk. When he saw me, he asked, 'Nali, where is your daughter now?'

'She is in London.'

'I am writing a poem for her.'

'What are you writing?'

'A Kannada poem from D.S. Karki. She should memorize this and recite it twice a day.'

'Bindu,' I said, 'she is busy with her routine. She won't be able to do it.'

'Don't tell me what is possible and what is not. Weren't you reciting the same poem four times a day?'

I thought about the days of the past. Yes, he was right. We followed his instructions blindly. His tone, style, modulations and perfect pronunciations had impressed us children so much that we had tried to memorize it in the same style and recite it in front of him for his approval. As I grew older, I started understanding and enjoying the richness of that literature. Even to this day, I enjoy reading it and feel proud of my heritage. My love for Kannada developed only because of him and not because of any books or teachers. I am glad that I was introduced to it at an early age. No matter what people said about him, I found his command over the subject to be wonderful.

In today's world, nobody cares for their neighbour's child. They don't spend a second or a rupee on other children unless it is advantageous for them. We were not Bindu's children, and he never gained anything from us. He didn't get any award for instilling a love for Kannada in us. And now, at this age, he was writing D.S. Karki's poem, *Please Light the Lamp of Kannada*, for my daughter. I absorbed love from him like a sponge and thanked him in my heart.

I consider him one of the most influential people from my childhood.

2

Jayant the Shopkeeper

In North Karnataka, most people of my parents' age were school or college teachers, postmasters, bank clerks or officers, or Life Insurance Corporation (LIC) agents. Doctors and engineers were rare. The generation after my parents boasted of doctors, engineers and chartered accountants. The current generation is vastly different; it prefers studying or settling abroad. Rarely in our community do people think of business. They fear the word itself.

Of all my cousins, Jayateertha was the only person who ventured into business by running a shop. Though his name was Jayateertha Shripad Rao Kulkarni, he was popularly known as Jayant the shopkeeper.

Jayant was very different from others even as a child. In school, he frequently bartered one thing for another.

He would take a mango from his garden and give it to his friend in exchange for a pencil, or tell his friend, 'I am not coming to school today. At home, I will say that the teacher is not there. Tomorrow, I will help you when you don't go to school.' He loved to make adjustments. When he went to college, he chose arts—not because he loved it but because he didn't want to work hard for commerce subjects, as it would keep him busy throughout the day. Science was out of his limits. The arts college had classes only in the morning, which would leave his afternoons free.

During these free hours, he would visit his friends' parents who ran small businesses and learned about entrepreneurial tricks. He would display his intelligence and learnings during dinner time at home. He would say, 'Mother, one chapati costs twenty-eight paise. One bowl of mango pulp costs forty paise. One glass of buttermilk costs thirteen paise.'

My grandmother believed that one must not equate money with food. The more food you give away, the better karma you get. She would get upset, 'Please keep quiet! Don't ever calculate how much we eat. After our death, we go to the court of Yama. He has a clerk called Chitragupta, who will punish us.'

'But why will he punish us?' I would unnecessarily butt in the conversation between *ajji* and Jayant.

'Chitragupta will say, "God gave you a human life so he will ask you the number of people you have fed."'

Grandmother would talk as if she was a witness in the court of the Lord of Death and Chitragupta was asking her about debit and credit accounts.

'At that time,' she would continue, 'if you say dinner costs so much, then he will put you in hell. You will suffer and regret the things you have done. People in hell will take a stick and hit you hard.'

Jayant would never show any emotion. But I would get scared, and say, 'Ajji, Jayant will never talk about food in terms of money again.' I would plead and she would agree to forgive him.

I was living in a small town that had no hotels at that time. If you knew someone, they would come directly to your home. It was a custom. There were no telephones, and you wouldn't have any advance information on visitor's arrivals. When people came for lunch, my grandfather would give them a glass of cool water from a clay pot covered by a wet cloth. He would also give them a little jaggery. He would inquire how they were doing and tell me, 'Nali, go inside immediately. Hurry up! Tell your grandmother to arrange for another plate for lunch.'

But he would turn towards the (sometimes restless) guest and say, 'I have told Nalini to hurry up, but not you. Please relax. Nalini's grandmother is old and needs some time to get things together.'

My grandfather would also say, 'It is afternoon. We are blessed. We have grains to eat and a lot of grandchildren who help. So, what is wrong with feeding our visitors and guests?'

He would enjoy people's company so much that he could easily start talking to any stranger. So, most of the time our guests would bring along their friends too. He always believed the more the merrier. Maybe that was the reason he brimmed with enthusiasm till he passed away at a ripe age.

My grandmother never objected or said, 'Oh no! I have to make extra food.'

Knowing her husband's nature, she almost always cooked extra food. She too believed that people must be fed properly. We children would help her with serving and cleaning. In case farmers came from the nearby village, my grandfather would tell my older cousins, 'Go inside and help your ajji in making additional rice and sambar.' He knew that farmers ate more since they would have travelled a long way. He would tell me, 'Go and fetch betel leaves and betel nut.' Those were the farmers' favourites. But Jayant remained unperturbed.

Jayant never believed in this philosophy of being generous with food. He would equate every meal with money. When I was alone, he would say, 'Today, five people were fed free of cost. What a loss!'

'No, three', I once replied, trying to be precise.

'You don't understand. Farmers eat more. One person eats for two. So, two farmers ate lunch. It is as good as four people. Plus, there was another guest. If you calculate each plate at two rupees, the lunch cost us ten rupees today. What a waste!'

It scared me when he brought up food and money in conversations. 'Don't be so loud, Jayant. Lord Yama will send you to hell, and I don't want you to go there or get beaten with a stick.'

Jayant would snigger.

Jayant's father was a postmaster who had a modest living with barely any ups and downs. He went to work at 8.30 a.m., took a break for lunch in the afternoon and then napped for an hour. He returned home around 5 p.m. In the evening, he would sit in the *verandah* and read out poetry to people who would gather there. There used to be at least twenty people in the audience every day, drawn by his good voice and oratorical skills.

Our job during these sessions was to serve buttermilk if it was summer and herbal tea during the winter.

When Jayant finished his Bachelor of Arts, no one took his plan to get into business seriously. Uncle advised him to become a schoolteacher in the same village. Jayant got upset. 'I will never become a schoolteacher,' he said. 'I can't look after so many children. There is no incentive to become one. I don't want a fixed salary and fixed timings. I want to be a businessman.'

'What is the meaning of a businessman?' granny asked.

'*Udyogapati.*'

'You can become *pati* of anything later but right now you become Uma pati,' she said.

Uma was uncle's best friend's daughter. She was a shy and well-behaved girl and granny liked her a lot.

Jayant danced with rage. I was reminded of Shiva's *tandav nritya*. 'There is no way I will marry Uma. First, I want to set up my business and second, she is a village girl. I want someone from the city.'

Everybody tried reasoning with him, but he did not budge an inch.

At last, tired, my grandfather said, 'Though nobody has done business or sold food grains in our family, if Jayant has decided that it is what he wants, then let him go ahead. Don't insist too much. After all, he is an adult. I will tell Uma's father to look for another boy.'

Later, Uma got married to a bank officer, who was transferred to Delhi. Uma joined her husband there and ironically, became the city girl that Jayant always wanted. During those days, migrating to a big city like Delhi was as good as going abroad.

Soon, Jayant started his business. Many elders advised him, saying, 'Jayant, business doesn't always ensure profit. Sometimes there's profit and sometimes loss. Not everyone can do business. You should have a knack for it. You must have a tough mind to give people loans to buy things, and you must be even tougher and smarter to recover those loans. In our house, we are not tough. You think it over.'

'Don't pull me down when I want to do something new. You should encourage me. Instead, you all are throwing negative thoughts my way. According to you, the people from our family should end up in the post office, bank or school. I will not accept such a fate.'

In a way, Jayant was right. No one encouraged him. However, that did not deter him. He started a grocery store after giving it careful thought. The family was known for being educated and feeding people—not for being wealthy. Jayant didn't have money to set up his store and so, he took a loan from the bank. He wanted his father's provident fund, but he had unmarried sisters and hence, his father refused to give him that. Jayant wrote the signboard for his shop in both English and Kannada—Shri Raghavendra Provision Store. Initially, the business went well. Jayant sat at the cash box and people would come and speak to him. The store was attached to the house. He would call from there, 'Nali, send a cup of tea for my customer.' His sister Shakku (Shakuntala), who is my cousin too, would help me when the orders gathered pace.

Within a fortnight, the tea powder, which should have lasted a month, was over and I was a little worried. 'Jayant, I think we have to stop offering tea to your customers. We are only two weeks into this month and the tea is over. You have to buy again,' I said.

'Nali, you will never understand. There is a new sales promotion technique. When customers come, you must make them feel relaxed and a cup of tea does that job. When you go to big sari shops in the cities like Mumbai, you are served cool drinks.'

I listened wide-eyed. I had neither seen Mumbai nor heard about such a service. But this new sales strategy became popular in his shop. Soon, word spread that if anyone went to Jayant's shop in the morning, they would certainly get free tea.

Many began to gather at Jayant's shop in the mornings. They drank tea, read the newspaper and left without buying anything.

One evening, I was at the temple, where I met my friend Malini. 'Nali,' she asked, 'how is Jayant's shop doing?'

'Well, I think. Many people come every day.'

'Nali, I heard my father talking. People just go there to have tea in the morning. Ten steps away, there is a provision store owned by Hebsur. It is an old store that is better than Jayant's in terms of prices. My dad also has tea at your shop but buys the provisions from Hebsur's.'

The other old stores in the area didn't use the new sales promotion technique. They also discouraged people from reading the newspapers unless they bought something. The conversations at these stores were brief and to the point. 'What do you need? Shall I charge it to your monthly account?' and so on. The owners of these stores knew the simple technique of management—high turnover gives high returns. Everyone in the family was a part of the business.

Poor Jayant neither had the advantage of a business-minded family nor the knowledge of the processes. His working style was different—he believed in friendly business. He would get up in the morning, listen to the radio, perform puja, read the newspaper, have breakfast and open the shop around 10.30 a.m., as if he was working in a post office or college. Hebsur's shop, on the other hand, was open by 7.30 a.m. Jayant would shut shop for lunch at 1.30 p.m. and reopen it around 4.30 p.m.

Once he had just shut the door when a customer, Raman, came running for tea powder. Too lazy to reopen, Jayant asked, 'Why do you want it now? It is not good to have tea at this time.'

'We have guests,' said Raman.

'Your guests should not have tea at this time.'

Raman was upset. 'Will you open the shop and give me tea or not?'

'Come at 5 p.m. I will give it to you then.'

Raman did not respond and went to Hebsur's shop. Satish, who was sitting at the cashbox and having his lunch, washed his hands and gave Raman the tea powder.

Raman said, 'There is no point going to Jayant's shop when I can walk into Hebsur's and get what I want any time.'

The news spread that Jayant is strict about timings. Better to go to Hebsur's shop, which is always open.

One day, Hussain sabi came to Jayant's shop to buy sugar. He did not have many clients and so he struck up a conversation.

Jayant said, 'You should buy jaggery and not sugar. It is better for health.'

Hussain said, 'Sir, those things we can discuss later. Right now, I need sugar, otherwise, my wife will get upset.'

Jayant continued speaking, 'Hussain, you should do the right things at the right time. You are asking for sugar at night. It is not good. Ask your mullah, even the time for namaz is fixed.'

Hussain didn't want to argue further so he left and bought the sugar from Hebsur's store. Again, rumour spread that Jayant doesn't do good business. He only wants to sell what he has, which might be old.

Customers stopped going to his store.

If there was any fight in the village, Jayant would close his store and be the first person to reach. He would soon take a side in the quarrel. However, other shopkeepers didn't take anyone's side and stayed in their store.

In the meantime, Jayant's sister Shakku's marriage was fixed. The wedding preparations soon started at his home. Special chefs arrived with their huge utensils and lots of sweets were prepared for the guests.

Jayant had a large heart. He told the cooks, 'Please don't worry. I have jaggery from Kolhapur, the best quality sooji from Belgaum and butter from Davanagere. I have only one sister. All the guests should remember the sweet for years to come. So, do it very well.'

When there was a shortage of grocery items, the cooks were allowed to enter the store and take what they needed. Jayant was too busy to monitor them and instead, was involved in the distribution of cards. In such weddings, Bindu was extremely hospitable. He would say, 'Please eat nicely. Don't feel shy. The sweets are made from the best quality ingredients. After all, they are all from Jayant's store. Eat more. Do you want to take it home for your children? We will pack it.'

He would turn to Jayant. 'Bring the best ghee from your shop. This is the time to be large-hearted.'

Jayant listened to him. With all these superlatives, the wedding went on well. When Jayant opened the shop after a week, it was empty along with his cash box. Everything had been spent without any accounting.

Banks started sending notices to collect their loan. Jayant went to many relatives' homes, but nobody helped because of their constraints and reasons. In the end,

Jayant's grandfather had to sell one of his rice fields to pay off the loan.

This would have never happened in others' stores. For instance, Jayant's friend Channa looked after Hebsur's shop. He would go to college, return to work and keep an account of every transaction. His father had told him, 'College is different. Business is different. To run a business, remember the following: don't be very friendly with customers. Once they become friendly, they may ask for credit, which they may or may not pay later. Usually, you can have credit with the postmaster or schoolmaster. They will repay. The Goddess of money is Lakshmi and there are many ways for her to walk away, but only one to stay with you, and that is respect. If you send any grocery from the store to your house, it must be charged to your personal account, and at the end of the month, it should be accounted for. To run a good business, you need to work hard and have an understanding of the customer. You must also open the shop as early as possible and close it as late as you can.'

Poor Jayant was unaware of such unsaid rules and only dreamed of profit.

He lost the money and sold the fields; the elders were upset. It left Jayant with no option but to shut down his business. Soon a nearby high school advertised for a vacancy. Jayant decided to take up this job. To qualify for that post, he pursued his bachelor in education through distance mode. He finally got that job and was also made a permanent employee. He married a girl from the city as per his wish, but to his surprise, she was very shy and orthodox. She adjusted well to village life.

Time went by. All the elders of the home passed away. Jayant's son became a software engineer and relocated to Bengaluru.

Jayant retired when it was time with a gratuity of Rs 10 lakh.

Despite all these years of teaching, people still referred to him as Jayant, the shopkeeper. His love for business prevailed deep in his mind. He had been unable to make any long-term entrepreneurial plans. The gratuity, however, sparked his desire once again—he decided to open a business again.

There were several advantages now. He had money and no elders to resist his plans. Though his wife repeatedly told him not to get into business, he didn't listen. Like most men, he ignored her and brushed her off, saying that she had not seen the world. He was firm on starting a new business.

He decided to open a gift centre this time around. Delighted with his new goal, he ran on to the street, much like Archimedes (unlike Archimedes, he wore his clothes!) to search for a shop on rent. He then felt that his old shop still held great value, and so, he reopened it. However, time had worn it out—it looked like a godown. A lot of old stuff had piled up, such as his grandmother's cradle, huge copper containers, water drums and remains from his previous business. It was quite a task to clean and paint it. He spent money on the revamp. He called it the Modern Gift Centre.

Jayant invited his friends and relatives for the inauguration. Snacks were arranged to lure them. People who attended the opening ceremony, spoke in a hush-hush manner. 'I hope this will not be history repeating itself,' some said. 'It doesn't look like a modern shop centre but like an old lady with make up,' others said.

He told everyone about his new pitch. 'We have articles that you can gift for all occasions, be it a wedding, housewarming, or a birthday. They are not very expensive, and my profits are marginal. Gift wrapping will be done for free.'

He distributed paper flyers advertising his store.

The first client was Shakku's husband. 'Jayant, my friend's son is getting married, and I want to give him a good gift.'

Jayant asked, 'What range?'

'Up to thousand rupees.'

Jayant chose steel kitchen sets, packed them and handed them over to him. When Shakku's husband came to the cash box, he said, 'Oh Jayant, I forgot to bring the wallet. I will send money through Shakku.'

Jayant felt uncomfortable but could not refuse. He looked at his wife and said, 'That is fine.'

Many relatives and friends came to his shop on that day, and everyone bought something or the other but very few paid. The reasons were different.

'My credit card expired yesterday. I will send money later.'

'I have less cash. I will pay later.'

For a sale of five hundred rupees, he received only fifty rupees.

But Jayant, who was brought up to be hospitable, was unable to ask these customers to let go of their purchase or pay up front. He could not change his nature.

Some of his old colleagues also came to his shop with reasons to stall payments. 'Jayant, three weddings are coming up. We can't afford to pay for all the purchases this time. You have known us for such a long time. We are pensioners. We will pay you every month, but please give us the three gifts right now.'

Jayant could not refuse.

However, money-related qualms did not end here.

A local girl, Surabhi, who lived in New York after her wedding, had come to meet her parents. She bought a wall clock from Jayant. However, the next day she returned it, saying, 'Your clock is not working. Return the money.'

'I have given the receipt, and once I issue it I don't refund, but you can buy something else for that money,' Jayant said.

'In America, I had once purchased a pressure cooker and used it for two days. I was not happy so the next day, I returned it to the shop and received a refund. You lag in customer service,' Surabhi argued.

'That is America, but this is not,' Jayant said in diffidence.

Thus, the gift centre's wares kept dwindling over the month along with his sales.

Jayant now began making rounds to collect the money owed to him by his customers. Shakku's husband said,

'Please come in. Sit down and relax. We will have some tea together.'

When he was about to ask for money, Shakku's husband said, 'I will come in the evening to pay. Don't worry.'

In every house, the story was different. Tea was given but money was not paid. Jayant waited for a week, but the money didn't come and accounts did not close.

He decided to undertake another round of collections.

As soon as he came, Shakku's husband said, 'Come Jayant, please keep chatting with your sister. I have some urgent work. Will try to return quickly.' Then, he went away.

So, he asked Shakku to pay for her husband's purchases. 'I don't know what my husband has bought. You didn't even ask me before giving the items to him. That business is between the two of you.'

Thus, Shakku slipped away.

And in this manner, Jayant's second round failed miserably, too. This time he wasn't even offered tea.

After two weeks, he went on a third round to collect money. Some people said, 'Jayant, life is not permanent. Why do you worry so much about money? Helping people is most important.'

Others gave sermons. 'Don't come here again and again for the sake of money. It doesn't suit your nature or your elders. You come from a family where your grandparents and parents would feed several people every day without any expectations.'

Within three months of its inauguration, Jayant's Modern Gift Centre closed permanently.

'Nali, I am really wrong. *Ajja* was right. If I had called four people and fed them, I would have at least been happy. Look at this—they take things from me and when I meet them, they blame me.'

'Where did you go wrong, Jayant?' I asked.

'I never received good training. And my mindset was not meant for this. Running your business sounds beautiful from the outside, but it requires tremendous work, and you must know how to get your money back. I have never in my life understood these two things. But look at Hebsur's shop. The business comes naturally to his children because they have seen it every day and they work harder than me. I have lost both money and my business.'

'What are you going to do now?' I asked him.

'I have a plan. My son and daughter-in-law are software engineers. Both go to work. Since both are working, they have to love their in-laws! We will go there and look after the house and the child.'

'This is another kind of business,' I understood and laughed.

3

Jealous Janaki

Janaki reminded people of a military commander. Tall, well-built and confident, she would attract attention wherever she went. Her eyes were sharp, her mind sharper and sharpest of all was her tongue. She would not fear anyone, but people were certainly scared to be in her presence.

As a young girl, I frequently visited her house because she would call me for errands, and I was too scared to disobey her. She used to take me along to buy things, as no one else would take up this task. Though her friend circle was limited, her acquaintances were many.

Once, we went to buy her chappals. We searched for a shop, but none of the chappals fit her. The shopkeeper suggested, 'Madam, I think you should try a gent's size.' That was enough for Janaki to pick up a fight.

She opened her mouth thunderously. 'What do you think? Do I look like a man to you? How dare you tell me that? I will see that your store is closed in no time. I will tell every woman that you disrespect their kind.' The threats went on and on.

The young salesman was in tears by the end of it. He said, 'Madam, I am sorry. You have very nice feet, but we don't have good enough chappals for you.'

She was smart enough to understand the real reason, so she nonchalantly walked over to the men's side and finally bought her slippers from there.

Janaki was married to Anant uncle, a high school teacher. Janaki had wanted a dynamic person, someone like her as her partner. She loved gossip, rumourmongering, misunderstandings, looking down on people and passing sharp remarks. Anant uncle was a quiet, studious and an extremely meek man.

Anant's students may or may not have feared him, but he was very scared of the principal. When he became the principal, he feared the teachers.

He always sought a second opinion on his work. At home, the terrorizing tigress Janaki never gave an opinion, but instead dictated her orders. She would boss him around.

'There is no rice or wheat flour. Go to the grocery shop and get some.'

'There are no vegetables. Call the vendor.'

'Go to the post office to see whether any registered post has come. I am expecting a letter today.'

'I have given my sari for ironing. Go bring it.'

Anant uncle became a meek student in front of the school monitor, Janaki.

Janaki was often compared to the All-India Radio for broadcasting the gossip from homes in our vicinity. Apparently, she knew the inside details of everyone's life. I think she should have been in the Central Bureau of Investigation. It would have been a great help to the country. Even without any training from Scotland Yard, she was a great detective. If you went to her house, there was always lots of unusual news about other families.

'It seems Advocate Joshi's son bagged the first rank in the university, but I have my own doubts. Joshi is a famous lawyer. He must have influenced the evaluation centre,' she once said.

'Come on, Janaki aunty. The exam is online. How can one imagine such a thing?' I said, summoning up my courage.

'There are many things that are not proven but you can guess with your common sense. Look at that boy— thin and tall. He looks like a patient. How can he get the first rank?'

'Janaki aunty, there is no relationship between brain and weight.'

She lowered her voice and said, 'He got more marks in viva, it seems. Now, don't ask me to prove it.'

Once Janaki aunty decided that something was the way she thought it is, it was final. Once, she remarked, saying, 'These days, girls have become very bold.'

'What is wrong with that?' I asked.

Janaki began explaining her logic, 'If women are bold, then there is no peace in the family. The husband and wife will fight all the time.'

'I don't agree with you at all,' I said. 'Economic freedom is one of the things that gives a woman her strength. Education makes her bold and enables her to stand up for her rights.'

Janaki aunty had forgotten that she was bold for her generation. Fortunately, Anant uncle was timid and so her family was peaceful. No one dared to argue with her because she was extremely assertive.

One day, my grandmother told me one of Janaki aunty's secrets. When Janaki aunty was young, she created a huge drama. Her mother-in-law was a quiet lady. During one of the festivals, she gave all her ornaments to Janaki to wear, who proceeded to the temple nearby to pray. Janaki returned home and started behaving funnily. She opened her hair and said, 'Goddess Amba has come to me.'

Everyone was scared. In those days, people believed that a God or Goddess can channel through a human and speak to the people.

Anant uncle, being weak-minded, prostrated immediately in front of her. 'O Goddess Amba! We are blessed that you have come to our house. What do you want? Have we made any mistakes? Please tell us your purpose.'

In a booming voice, Janaki declared, 'Your daughter-in-law is a very good person. If you keep her happy, the family will be happy. Whatever you have offered her today must remain with her permanently.'

Her mild mother-in-law wanted to say something, but Anant uncle stopped her. 'Don't speak, mother. This is the Goddess' decision, and we must abide by it.'

She asked for good food and slept with all the jewellery on her that day. From then on, she kept all the jewellery to herself.

The next morning, she woke up and behaved as if nothing had happened. This is how she was famously known for managing anything, anytime, anywhere.

When she got married, she was only sixteen years old. She did not have a father. Her stepbrothers took away all her mother's assets. Her mother raised Janaki without help. She was the one who found Anant uncle, and the marriage was fixed without much hassle. But to their surprise, in a couple of years, Janaki grew taller than Anant uncle. That's the reason the couple hardly went out together.

They had two sons, who obeyed their mother. They couldn't afford to offend her. They were well-educated and well-mannered.

Anant uncle would leave for school by 10 a.m. and around the same time, their sons headed to their work. Janaki aunty would cook and pack their lunches as they would only return by 5.30 p.m. She would finish all her chores by 10.30 a.m., and that's when she would begin hunting for exciting 'news'.

She would hear the news from all around and spread it in the neighbourhood. She would take action based on the gossip. She shunned advice, did not believe in verifying facts or think about the consequences of her actions.

Sometimes she would go to many houses during the day and return only in the evening. Janaki would also visit my grandmother's house. She was a little scared of my strict grandmother, who had no tolerance for gossip. My grandmother, Krishna, knew that Janaki, who tormented others, feared her to an extent.

'Janaki, control your tongue. What you talk about and what you eat are most important. What you say makes you what you are,' my grandmother told her.

Janaki would neither reply nor did she care much.

Every morning, Janaki would get up, do minimal work, sit in the verandah and read the newspaper accompanied by loud commentary. Neighbours did not need to buy the paper owing to her narrations.

'Oh, Raghu's photo has come in the paper! He is a social worker. I have known Raghu ever since he was born. What social work does he do? He wears *khadi* clothes, has a *jhola* and spends time with the children. That's all. Is it social work? He must have paid money or put his own advertisement in the newspaper.'

'Oh, see? Kusuma Bai's photo is also there. What has she done for this? Oh, it is a story that she has written. I know Kusuma's ex-boyfriend and present husband, etc. Maybe she has written her own biography.'

'Oh, I see Godavari's wedding invitation in the newspaper. Why is that in the paper? Must be an urgent marriage. No time to distribute the cards. I hope, both my sons will not give such trouble to me.'

Initially, Anant uncle said, 'Why do you comment unnecessarily and talk ill of people without knowing the facts? The morning time is peaceful. Take God's name, read something nice.'

Later he stopped it because his well-intentioned advice did not affect her.

In the afternoon, she would dress well, tie her hair, adorn it with jasmine flowers, and meet her husband on their house's threshold. 'The morning's chapatis are left over. I ate at Jayant's house. I am in a hurry. The rice is in the cooker. Yoghurt is in the fridge. Please add *tadka* to the sambhar. Have your lunch. Keep the remaining food on the table. I will return in the evening and cook some vegetables.' Saying this, and without waiting for his response, she would go off to a temple.

Anant uncle knew she won't return before the night. So, he would cook a vegetable, eat and read a book.

When I look back now, I feel bad for Janaki. There was no WhatsApp during those days. Poor one, she had to go from house to house to deliver what she thought was news.

There was only one person, the church attender's wife, Mariamma, who loved Janaki immensely. She openly said, 'Let people say whatever they want about Janaki. The kind of courage she has, I don't think anyone else in this town has.'

Mariamma supported her argument with an instance.

'The other day, my husband went to church for work and did not return for two days. I was scared. The church is away from the city, and we have a lot of land. Our doors are not strong. I was with baby Shashikala. It was a moonless night. I called Yesudas, our helper in the church, to sleep in our home, but that fellow got drunk and didn't show up.'

'Mariamma, what did you do? There is a tamarind tree in your compound. I have heard that ghosts live on those trees,' I asked her in apprehension.

'Nali, even I was scared. I locked the house and went to Janaki's home. By then, she knew that Yesu was drunk, and that my husband was not in town. She was getting ready to visit me. I don't know how she had got this message.'

'Janaki said, "Don't get scared, Mariamma. I will come to your house and sleep there for the night."'

She slept in Mariamma's house that night.

'I want to tell you a secret, Nali. My husband gets more scared than I do whenever there is an unknown noise outside our home. But when Janaki was home, I slept like a log the entire night. I know that no ghost or man will dare to come to our house when she is around. Whatever you say, we require people like Janaki in this town.'

Janaki aunty's greatest quality is that when someone is in difficulty, she goes out of her way to help him or her. If somebody is fighting and they see Janaki coming, they will immediately quieten down because they know that she won't spare anyone. Sometimes I think she should have joined the police force. She would have been a great superintendent of police.

If there is a death, irrespective of the community, Janaki is one of the first to show up. She will send food for the next two days. She will avoid visiting the temple on those days. She gives enormous moral strength. That may be the reason people don't want to fight with her.

The other day, I saw Janaki going somewhere. I knew that her time of return was unpredictable, so I made some sambar rice to give to Anant uncle before he started cooking. When I took it to his home, old Anant uncle had put on lights in front of God and was praying.

Though I am old now, his affection for me has not reduced.

'Nali, come. I am seeing you after many days,' he said. 'Since you got married you have barely visited us. How are you? How is your mother-in-law?'

'Everything is fine, kaka. But the house feels so empty when Janaki aunty is not home. Tell me, how do you spend your time when she roams around till late like this?'

Kaka smiled. With a steady voice, he said, 'I feel bad for her.'

'Why kaka?'

'She is bold and bright with a great memory. She has tremendous creativity and enormous energy. It has to be dissipated somewhere. She did not have proper schooling, and the entire energy was diverted into many parts. Hence, she doesn't have peace of mind. If she concentrates, she can learn many new things, but she doesn't. She has no misplaced intentions or bad values, but she wastes her energy on the wrong things. It is better that I am at peace.'

I am surprised how Anant uncle had understood his wife's mind and still happily lived with her.

4

Ganga the Unadaptable

Our town believed that Ganga was exceptionally beautiful. One could say that she was blessed with beauty that could win hearts across the nation. She was tall, had long hair, beautiful eyes and a clear complexion, and she carried herself elegantly.

When she was around twenty years old, several suitors approached her parents asking for her hand in marriage.

Apart from her beauty, she was also intelligent. She had done her BA, read novels regularly and knew Hindi, embroidery and knitting. She was aware of her beauty and talents—that made her arrogant.

Ganga had a brother, Shiva, who was her exact opposite. He lacked a well-rounded education, was not well-spoken and was not particularly good-looking. He was a traditional farmer, who was happy in his own circle of friends. Ganga always looked down upon him and others—she would often make unpleasant comments about them.

'Meeru is so ordinary in her looks. I don't know if anyone will be able to like her.'

'Subhash's features are so bad that he can become a joker in a movie.'

'Vishnu is okay, but not marriage material.'

She was never short of such loose comments.

Once, there was a wedding in the next town. Ganga called my mother and said, 'Send Nalini with me for two days. I am going to attend a wedding.'

It was common that neighbours often called upon schoolchildren, who were on their holidays, to attend weddings and help at the temples and festivals. I gladly went with Ganga.

Even at the wedding venue, the bride paled when compared to Ganga. Everybody wanted to speak to Ganga and ask her about her long, lovely hair.

Ganga became dramatic because of the attention she received. 'It is God's gift,' she said, 'everyone cannot have it. You have to look after it a lot. I need another person to hold my hair during a head bath. I shampoo on top and the other does the end. I use oil which has powder of red hibiscus, and I always dry my hair in the shade. Everybody looks with great awe.'

We had a good dinner that night.

Moments later, a handsome young man, who was among the attendees, brought me a box of chocolates and said, 'This is for you'.

It was great fun to have an entire chocolate box to myself without sharing it with anyone. Then he started speaking to me, 'What is your name? I am Subhash.'

As an innocent young kid, I didn't understand that the chocolate box was a bribe to learn more about Ganga.

'Nalini,' I said.

'With whom have you come here?'

Without a moment's hesitation, I opened the box, took a chocolate and pointed to Ganga.

'Is she your sister?'

I reached out for another chocolate and unwrapped it. 'Yes, kind of,' I said, diplomatically.

'When are you going?'

'Tomorrow or the day after.'

'Which town are you from?'

I gave the name of my town, the address of my house, Ganga's house and a landmark.

I noticed something very unusual. The handsome man was looking at Ganga all the time.

Soon, Ganga noticed that I was done with half a box of chocolates. She was upset when I explained who had given it and the questions he had asked. 'Nali, why did you take this box and why did you give information?'

'I don't know. He asked and I gave,' I continued.

When we were returning by bus, I saw the same man and told her, 'Look Ganga, Subhash is also coming on the same bus.'

Ganga just smiled as if she was expecting it.

The next day, Subhash asked her parents for Ganga's hand in marriage, but Ganga refused. Her mother came and told my mother, 'The boy is very good, but you know Ganga is a peculiar girl. She feels his job isn't that great and that he is not very well off. She also feels that he doesn't deserve a wife like her. We keep telling her she has very high standards for her groom.'

Most of the time, Ganga would reject the boys— different boys for different things. She wanted someone very handsome, rich, with no parents and somebody who would listen to her unflinchingly. Nobody fulfilled her criteria. The elders at home explained to her that it was not necessary that all orphans should be good-looking and wealthy; it's better to have in-laws who can guide you through difficulties. But nothing would get into her head.

Bindu told her, 'If you were born five hundred years ago during the Vijayanagara era, maybe Emperor Krishna Deva Raya would have married you for your virtues and looks. But remember that he was not good-looking either. He was short.'

Ganga got up and left.

At last, she liked a boy, Satish. He was a well-qualified doctor, who met her criteria. But, she received the first shock of her life when he rejected her. How could any man reject someone like her? she thought. The reason he gave was very logical. 'I would like to marry a girl who is a doctor. She can possibly help me in my work,' he had said.

Ganga could not imagine that a doctor's education was more important than her beauty. When she attended his wedding, she commented, 'I understand why Satish does not deserve a wife like me. His taste is so poor that he has married a lady with a crow's face. That is life.'

Her bar for a groom only went higher after Satish's rejection. She wanted to marry a boy better than him. And so, she kept turning down the proposals that followed.

'Oh, he is as tall as a coconut tree; I can't even speak to him properly.'

'He is so short like a Lilliputian. I have to look down upon him every time.'

'He looks like a coolie.'

'This fellow does not have his own house. Is he going to live like Lord Shiva in the cremation ground?'

'This guy looks like a villain or a wrestler.'

'That fellow is born on a new moon day. It is not good for the wife.'

The list of reasons grew longer.

Even the ever-optimistic Bindu tried to reason with her but failed miserably. He said, 'Ganga cannot marry anyone.' Janaki stated, 'I can't bring a daughter-in-law like Ganga. She would spend half her time and 70 per cent of her husband's salary on her beautification.'

Ganga only grew older amid the string of rejections.

Her parents passed away. Shiva, her brother, who had been postponing his wedding for his sister, at last asked her to keep on waiting for her prince charming and that he wished to marry an ordinary girl as he was a simple person. Shiva went on to marry a girl named Girija.

Soon, Ganga started picking fights with Girija. The latter kept quiet for a while, but later, she rebelled. Ganga would hit below the belt with her comments like, 'Some animal has entered our family.'

One day, Girija retorted, saying, 'It is nice to have beauty, but beauty with arrogance is a bad quality. I cannot stay with you anymore.'

Thus, the property was divided between Shiva and Ganga, with Ganga getting maintenance money every month.

As more years went by, age streaked across Ganga's face. Her long, luscious hair had started greying and thinning. Wrinkles formed across her cheeks and dark circles developed under her eyes. She was unable to retain her youthful beauty despite her best efforts. The people she had rejected were now quite well-settled in life. Subhash had opened a factory in Bengaluru and led a good life. Satish and his wife were well-known surgeons in India.

Ganga increasingly became bitter. To ward off her loneliness, Shiva brought the proposal of a good farmer from a neighbouring district. The boy said, 'I want a wife who will help me to look after the fields as I have two hundred acres of land. There is a lot of work.'

Ganga did not agree, 'I don't want to stay in a village and be in the fields all the time. My beauty will be affected. I am ready to marry him if he agrees to move to the city.'

The farmer replied, 'Sorry, I can't. I love my land. If a woman puts such conditions before marriage, then I don't want her.'

46

Shiva thought, 'If only Ganga had less beauty, she might have been normal.'

Now, Ganga had plenty of time and no one to talk to. She was always upset either with Shiva or Girija and would often pick fights with neighbours.

Sometimes, she would cry. At first, people felt sorry for her, but nobody could help her, knowing her personality.

Then one day, Girija said to my mother, 'There is a boy in Bengaluru. When he was young, he had polio because of which he developed a slight limp. He has a good job and no parents. He is keen to marry Ganga. Will you talk to her about it?'

My grandmother called Ganga to our home. I was married by then.

I wanted to tell her that a marriage or a relationship requires compromise on both sides. Looks don't remain the same. Romance and attraction fade with time, too. However, I refrained from giving her this advice as she was older to me, and I felt she might get hurt. However, my grandmother gave her a sermon and told her the analogy of the river Ganga, who is born in the Himalayas but ultimately adjusts to the ocean in the Bay of Bengal.

'River Ganga is respected today because she feeds millions of people,' my grandmother explained. 'To do that, she has adjusted a lot—from hills to plains, plains to ocean. If she would not have adjusted, then she would have flowed in some desert and disappeared.'

However, Ganga rejected outright the proposal of the well-to-do man with a slight limp.

'Tell Girija that when her daughter grows up, will she get her a groom who limps? There is no way I can marry a handicapped person.'

Ganga stopped coming to our home the day after my grandmother tried to advise her. Later, my mother found another boy. He came to meet Ganga along with his parents.

Ganga rejected the older brother and preferred the younger one who was already engaged. She said, 'The older brother looks like a father. I can't marry an old man.'

And so, Ganga remained unmarried.

One evening, Ganga sent some sweets to our home. Innocently I asked, 'What is the occasion?'

Shiva said, 'Some groom came to meet Ganga so this was prepared. I don't think Ganga will agree to this. She is used to living alone, making comments and being bitter around everybody.'

I sat on a stone bench outside, remembering the wedding I had attended with Ganga when she was young and then thought of today's scenario. What a great difference! But Ganga had remained the same.

My grandmother once said, 'You don't remain young for long. The window for marriage can be very small for women in this society. Nobody gets the perfect husband of their dreams. If the fundamentals are fine and values match, then you simply have to adjust the rest. We all believe that life is beautiful beyond marriage. Actually, life starts after marriage. Even if you marry a prince, it is not necessary that life will be easy. Princess Sita married the great prince Ram. What did she get in the end? Draupadi married five great warriors and she suffered so much still. Ganga should understand that acceptance and adjustments are the basics of marriage.'

I don't know whether Ganga learnt this lesson, but I was surely amazed by my grandmother's words and experiences.

5

Hema the Woman Friday

Hema would never be found in her home. She was always in somebody else's home, helping its members through their crises, or occasions such as childbirths, deaths or weddings.

The other day, Amba had a baby girl after ten years of marriage. Her husband and her mother-in-law were indeed very happy, but they did not know how to take care of the newborn and the new mother. Because of her age, Amba's mother-in-law couldn't help much. Her husband was busy calling everyone and sharing the news, rather than tending to the mother and child.

Finally, Amba's mother-in-law told her son, 'Enough of making calls now! First call Hema. She will advise us on what to do next. I can't run around as I am old.'

Before she could complete the sentence, Hema arrived.

'Arrey Hema, how did you know? I was just telling him to call you,' said the old woman. She was relieved at the mere sight of Hema. She was assured that her daughter-in-law and granddaughter were safe in Hema's hands.

'Someone told me that Amba was admitted to the hospital. Then I remembered that only the two of you were at home. So, I came here as soon as I could. I know that you will soon be swamped with work. You don't have to call me to ask for help. I have made a list of what all we need to do next.'

Saying thus, Hema swung into action.

'First, you call Bundle Bindu. I know he doesn't do much work, but he has a good rapport with people. I will tell him to arrange for some sweets and chocolates to be delivered to your house. You will have to distribute it among the young and old. We will also call Ganga home; she will do neat and decorative packing of gifts. I can also ask her to keep a few things ready to receive the mother and child, once they are discharged from the hospital. Is it a normal delivery or a C-section? I have to plan her post-delivery care based on it. And also call Nali. She is quite sharp and will be helpful to me in many ways.'

Within a few minutes, I was there and ready to assist Hema aunty.

She opened her bag to show me. 'Look, I have brought some old clothes and an old blanket for the baby.'

'Hema aunty, why have you brought such old things for the baby?' I asked. 'Look at the things Amba's husband has brought.'

He had dragged in a big bag of new clothes.

'No, Nali. A newborn can't wear unwashed clothes. Their skin will be very sensitive. It might cause rashes or allergies. A child that has just come out of the mother's womb must be wrapped in a comfortable cloth to impart the same sense of warmth and feeling she had felt in the womb.'

'How did you know that?' I was curious.

'When you were born, I had done the same. And when you have a baby, I will do the same again. Just stop questioning me and help me with my work.'

Thus, Hema aunty put a stop to my questions and assigned me work. Hema aunty and Amba aunty were not related. But in a small town like ours, we lived like a family. We have taken great pride in such bonding and have felt happy being together during each other's time of need.

Hema aunty was in charge for the next sixteen days— the sixteenth day being the child-naming ceremony. Everybody was aware of her depth of knowledge and so, nobody questioned her. She commanded great respect and was like an untiring captain leading an army.

'Nali, anyway you are on vacation now. Come here every day. You can have lunch here and go home by evening. Take a pencil. Write down the list of cooks to be called.'

'How about Swami?' I suggested. Hema dismissed the recommendation unceremoniously, 'No, no! Rasam is the index of cooking. He doesn't make it tasty.'

'Venkat then?'

'He makes good rasam, but his laddoos are too mushy.'

I was no match for her intelligence or experience.

Then she said, 'Call Krishna. Though he is a little slow at work, the quality and taste of his food are very good.' I turned around and ran to Krishna's house.

If you really want to see Hema aunty in full form, then a wedding is the best place. Usually, both wedding parties have great expectations and misunderstandings often occur. Everybody has an agenda, except the bride and the groom. They have relatives waiting for any opportunity to take advantage of the situation and start a Kurukshetra-like war.

At weddings, apart from a flurry of emotions—happiness, sadness, anxiety—there is work to be done.

Hema aunty dealt with complex situations with her memory, speech and leadership qualities. She would be everywhere—overseeing the kitchen, counting gifts, preparing *akshata* (sacred rice used in auspicious occasions) and entertaining guests. Those times I remember the meaning of the word omnipresent.

The other day, it was my cousin Sridevi's wedding. I met Hema in the market. She was as ecstatic as if she had won the lottery. She called out to me. 'Nali, come here quickly.'

I ran to her.

'Nali, you are in college now. But that doesn't mean you can stop helping me. You know Sridevi is getting married?'

'Of course, I know. She is my cousin. But why are you sounding so excited? What are you doing here?'

She showed me the list in her hand. 'I am here to invite the bangle seller home as per our custom. I also have to place the order with the flower vendor and give her the invitation card. I am telling her not to bring only jasmine but also roses and a few other varieties of flowers.'

The grown-up me had grown-up kind of questions now.

'Hema aunty, why are you tiring yourself so much? Sridevi has a sister-in-law, Chabbi (also known as Chhaya). Her family is also there to assist her. They will do all of this.'

'Stop it, Nali,' she said in a hushed tone. 'Chabbi is very upset for some reason and has gone to her mother's place. Today her husband has gone to bring her back. Poor Rama, Sridevi's mother, can't do all the work and I felt sorry for her.'

'Are they paying you?' I asked her.

'Maybe they are. Maybe they are not. I don't ask and I don't expect.'

That was Hema aunty. I really didn't understand her. Earlier, middle-class families didn't outsource the planning of a wedding to an organizer. The entire house would participate in arranging things. But things changed gradually. Hema aunty didn't understand modern economics or sociology and remained enthusiastic about every wedding as if it were her daughter's. People took advantage of her enthusiasm and got their work done. Most of the time they didn't pay her. And yet, Hema aunty didn't mind at all.

I saw Hema the day before the wedding. The bride's mother, Rama, had given her the key to the jewellery locker. Hema was counting the ornaments and depositing them in the safe. While she did so, she kept speaking. 'Now, I will give you money whenever you need it. I have counted and kept an account. All the wedding sarees are here too but the keys are with me.'

Then she saw me and Ganga. She called us, 'Have you seen the gift given to Sridevi by her mother?'

Ganga wasn't interested and neither was I, but she went on. She opened the cupboard and showed us two saris. 'See this red Banarasi sari is from her mother and this yellow Kanchi is from her brother. The remaining sari count is in my purse. I should update it now.'

She continued, 'You know her uncle had bought her a *tanmani* (a kind of pear famous in Maharashtra) necklace from Pune. It is beautiful. Whatever said and done, I always believe that Pune pearls are very good.' Then she closed the cupboard. Hema aunty knew the details of everything.

We followed her to the storeroom, where she started taking out utensils. She said, 'This container should go to the boy's side. Nali, take it to them.'

'Why should we give the better container to them and the ordinary one to the girl's side, Hema aunty?' I asked, lessons in equality playing on my mind.

'Nali, you don't understand. Till now, the son has been dependent on his mother, and she is used to his attitude. After the wedding, he will depend on his wife. It is hard for a woman to digest such a change. While the boy's mother is happy about her son's wedding, she also feels a loss, thinking that her son will now become somebody's husband. That's the reason she may get a little upset. I want to soothe her with these small things.'

'Hema aunty, I don't agree with you. If a boy's mother is losing her son, the girl's parents are also losing their daughter,' I said.

'Nali, the girl knows that she will go to the boy's house after the wedding. She is mentally prepared. You don't understand.'

I didn't understand how a better container could make any mother-in-law feel better. Then I remembered that Hema aunty belonged to an older generation, and I should pardon her. I shouldn't throw my gender equality statements on her.

Later, she sat and started making tea. 'The best tea should go to the boy's mother. Hurry up!' she ordered me.

This time I did not ask any questions.

For the next two days, people approached Hema aunty for work. She also secretly carried messages from the girl to the boy.

Just when everything was going smoothly, a dramatic situation arose.

The boy's uncle was a nasty person. He was looking for reasons to pick up fights. Such people exist at every wedding.

He said, 'Oh, we were not respected. Nobody called us first.'

Hema was asked to mitigate immediately. She said, 'I am sorry. It is my mistake. They told me to invite all of you first, but I forgot.'

I knew that it wasn't true, but Hema aunty was ready to put aside her ego for the sake of peace during the wedding.

When the wedding was over, Sridevi left with her husband. Then, Hema aunty became busy in handling the remaining items and handing over the charge back to Rama aunty. 'Look, this is the cash, and these are the gifts remaining from the wedding. These many laddoos are left too. I have locked the locker and here is the key. Now, I want to go.'

Rama aunty thanked her profusely and even Chabbi was very happy with Hema aunty's work and dedication. However, while people were admiring her, she was already thinking about her husband's dinner. She walked out empty-handed.

I next saw Hema aunty when Shyam Rao, our neighbour, died of a heart attack. He had two sons and one daughter, all of whom had settled abroad. Only his wife, Rukmini, was present at the time of death. We were woken up at 4 a.m. by Hema aunty's voice.

My grandmother went to help as well. I followed her. Rukmini was sitting, dumbstruck. Hema aunty kept on saying, 'Please take courage, Rukmini. As they say in Sanskrit, "*anayase na maranam*". Let me die without troubling anybody.'

She turned to look at me and said, 'Nali, what is the second half?'

'*Vina daynaya Jeevanam*,' I completed. It means to live a life without asking anything of anybody.

Hema aunty continued, 'You must have courage. You and your husband were not born together and do not go together. It is the law of life. First, let's call your children.'

By then, Bundle Bindu had also arrived.

'Bindu, go and make further arrangements. Rukmini, your nephew is here,' said Hema Aunty. 'You decide whether you would like to arrange for keeping the body for a night or would you like to cremate today?'

She left the room for them to talk.

Then it was my grandmother's turn to console her.

This time I didn't ask Hema aunty how she had arrived here.

Rukmini's children decided on the next course of action and things went on as usual.

Hema aunty visited their home continuously for ten days.

In the end, the children thanked Hema aunty in their American accent. 'Without you, things would have been so difficult. Thank you.'

One of them said, 'Why does this lady come here every day? It is our family matter.'

Rukmini stopped her children from uttering one more word.

Janaki said, 'If Hema was not there, nothing would have moved in your house. It is not a western family where individuality is of great importance or family means only husband, wife and children. This is North Karnataka, where we consider helping in difficult times a kind of puja to God. You should be grateful to her.'

After Janaki's monologue, Bindu couldn't hold back. 'This is the Kannada culture of North Karnataka where families are connected.'

The Americanized children's faces fell.

Over the years, Rukmini, Rama aunty and Sridevi forgot about Hema aunty's help at difficult junctures in their lives. As she comes uninvited, they didn't value what she offered, but Hema aunty never minded it.

A few years later, I got to hear one more instance of Hema aunty's generosity, narrated by Mulla sabi, who I crossed paths with at the town's dargah. He had a bag filled with mangoes. When he saw me, he said, 'Nali akka, I have to go for my labour work, and I don't have time. Will you hand over this bag to Hema aunty?'

'Why Mulla sabi? Did she visit your house too?'

'Yes, my bibi had a difficult delivery. Hema aunty took a vow before God and told me to take her to the government hospital. My bibi ended up delivering our child through a C-section. That saved her life, and we now have a wonderful baby girl.'

'What did she pray for?'

'She prayed in front of my bibi. She said, "If Mulla sabi's wife has a safe delivery, then I will give twenty mangoes to God." Why should she spend for the mangoes? So, I have bought them and want to send them to her.'

He continued, 'It is very hard to find people like her in life. Neither my wife nor I have mothers. She has been sending rice, rasam and other food items for my wife every day since her delivery. She also sent old clothes and cow's ghee. We don't know how to make it. My bibi is a great cook. She makes great surkumba (a dish similar to payasam), and chicken dishes. Hema aunty has told her not to eat meat for three months. Eat only vegetarian food, take an iron tablet, go to the hospital and take vaccinations as needed.'

Saying this, Mulla sabi handed me the mangoes and left.

I went home, took a sari and cash of five thousand rupees. By then I was no longer a young Nali, but an earning member, who could make independent decisions.

I went to Hema aunty's home. She was helping her husband prepare for the puja and making a garland for Lord Hanuman. She looked old and a little bent but was as cheerful as ever. When she saw me, she said, 'O Nali, why have you come here all the way? You could have sent word and I would have come.'

'Why Hema aunty, shouldn't I come to your house?' I said in a protesting voice.

'Not like that Nali,' she hesitantly said, 'I have a small house like Sudama. I am not like Krishna.'

'Your heart is large. Come on Hema aunty. I am not Krishna, and you are not Sudama. And your house is very neat.'

'So, what is special today, Nali?'

'Nothing aunty. Why should I come only for work? You are such a good human being. You helped my mother when I was born. You helped me when I gave birth to my child. You have been a part of our family in birth and death. I just thought I should come and say thank you.'

I gave the gifts and the mangoes and told her they were from Mulla sabi.

Suddenly I saw tears well up in Hema aunty's eyes. I had never seen her cry.

'Did I say something wrong aunty?' I asked, concerned. 'I am sorry if I hurt you.'

'No, Nali. I was crying out of happiness. There is somebody who cares about me. I like to help people, so I work for them. I get happiness by helping others. They don't care about me. In any wedding, hundreds of kilos of sweets are made but after the wedding, nobody says, "Hema, take a few to your home." They don't even bother whether I have had my dinner or not. Many times, I have come home, drank buttermilk and slept because I was just too tired. They leave their locker keys with me, but they don't have a heart big enough to give me even a small gift. Normally, the leftover and inexpensive saris are given to me.'

'In that case, why do you help them? If they think that you are so cheap, you should stop doing that.'

'Nali, I have a principle. I am not well educated, and I don't know much about philosophy, but I have learnt that we get a human life with great difficulty. You could have been easily born as a dog or a cat or a mosquito. When you are born a human, don't expect anything from anyone. But help others when they are in need. And I live by that.'

I was amazed at her simple yet profound philosophy, which even many swamis and gurus perhaps do not comprehend entirely. Philanthropy doesn't always mean giving money. Helping others without expecting anything in return and at times, getting negative remarks and continuing the work is real philanthropy. In my view, Hema aunty is one of the best philanthropists I have ever met.

I bowed my head and touched her feet.

6

Not Made for Each Other

It was well known in our town that Banabhatta and Parvati were not made for each other. If there were a competition called 'not made for each other', they would have won the first prize. This despite Banabhatta himself being an astrologer-cum-priest. He had matched their horoscopes and they had aligned well. His predictions were correct, except when it came to himself.

'Everyone had an opinion on this matter. Even history says . . .' said Bindu without any proof.

'Who knows, Parvati might not have given her original horoscope,' said Ganga.

'If they were in America, they would have got a divorce in a month,' said Janaki, who had never been to America. 'Because it was so obvious that they are unfit to be man and wife.'

Parvati had an amiable personality and was good-looking. She dressed well and always appeared neat. Banabhatta, on the other hand, was shabby. His dhoti and stole were always stained. His front teeth had reddened from habitually ruminating on paan. He sported two earrings, which added to his unattractiveness. He had an oily face with pimples. And since he ate out every day—at weddings, birthdays, *satyanarayana* pujas and *shraddhas*—his tummy had become big and bulging. He did not shave daily owing to superstitions about stars and the days (on which one could and could not shave). As a result, he resembled a clown.

People say that opposites attract but in Parvati's and Banabhatta's case, the opposites repelled.

I would frequent Parvati's home when I was a child. She had come to our town from a neighbouring one. Whenever there was a festival in our house, she would come and help my grandmother in the kitchen. My grandmother had a superlative appreciation for her work.

'So neat!'

'So good.'

'There is nobody like Parvati in the entire town.'

Initially, I was a messenger between my family and Parvati's as there were no phones during those days. Later, I became her friend. One afternoon, I went to her house. Large-hearted Parvati said, 'Come and have lunch.'

Seeing a clean plantain leaf, I sat down in front of it. Parvati came running up to me and said, 'Nali, get up. Don't sit there! This is my leaf and I have just finished my lunch.'

I had unknowingly sat at the leaf from which she had eaten. When I looked on the opposite side, I could see the contents of Banabhatta's leaf. One-third of the rice had spilled over, and sambar was flowing down. There was leftover chapatti.

Her kitchen was like a lab, very neat. She had ten different towels, all in different colours.

'What are these, Parvati?'

'Nali, the first one is for wiping hands. The second is for wiping the vessels. The third is for cleaning the vegetables. The fourth I use while making chapatis. And the last one is for wiping the kitchen counter.'

She didn't have any acrylic or plastic transparent containers but brass vessels that she had labelled with stickers. She had a statue of Annapoorna on the counter. It was minimally decorated and there was a small fruit placed in front of it.

'What is this, Parakka?' I asked affectionately. She liked it when I called her Parakka.

'I consider this to be my work field, and Goddess Annapoorna should bless what I cook. Every day I pray to her and then start my cooking,' she said.

Unlike her, Banabhatta was always in a hurry. In the morning, he would run to the Shiva temple as he was a hereditary priest. After 10 a.m., he would rush to perform ceremonies somewhere. After noon, he would hurry to nap and, in the evening, he dashed to the temple for some work. When there was no work, he would distribute sweets among the children. That would make him late, prompting him to speed towards his next task. This hastening had earned him the name of *Gadibidi* Bhatta. Gadibidi in Kannada translates to hurry burry.

'The other day,' Janaki said in a hush-hush tone, 'it seems he went to somebody's funeral and forgot to order the wood.'

'O you don't know? Bhatta is quite a dangerous person. It seems that in some weddings, instead of giving mangalasutra to the boy so that he can tie it around the bride's neck, he was about to do it himself in a hurry,' exaggerated Bindu.

'He may want to marry a second time,' said Ganga.

Hema stopped everyone. 'All of you, won't you keep quiet? Don't exaggerate, Bindu. Everybody has their own worries.'

Janaki had another question. 'Hema, tell me if they had had children—do you think they would have fought more or less?'

Ganga said, 'They would have fought more on how to raise them.'

'A child would have united them, I think,' said Hema.

Parvati's and Banabhatta's daily routines were also different. Parvati would get up around 6 a.m. She liked to have a cup of tea and read the newspaper before taking a shower.

Bhatta's routine was a contrast. He had to get up at 4.30 a.m. at *Brahmi muhurta*, which is supposed to be a very auspicious time to start the day. He had a cold-water bath irrespective of season, applied *vibhuti* (holy ash)—

probably more than what lord Shiva applies on himself—wore a *rudraksh* mala and did Shiva *panchakshari*, a special hymn in praise of lord Shiva. He would punctuate the mornings with his chants, '*Shiva mahatame*', while performing puja at home and then run to the temple.

Parvati liked to prepare different things for breakfast. She would read cookbooks and experiment—sometimes she would make north Indian dishes like parathas, sevaiyya, upma, and on others, she would cook Mangalore Kotta.

Banabhatta refused to eat these dishes. 'How can you eat all that for breakfast?' he would say. 'It is not in our scriptures. My mother never cooked all this. I must eat traditional food—rice, chapati, sambar, vegetable and yogurt. And for breakfast, upma or poha. The rest are forbidden.'

Whenever Parvati attempted a new breakfast item, she would send me word. I was a regular visitor at her house for breakfasts. I would diligently share opinions on her culinary skills. Slowly, I became a little friend to her. Sometimes, she would try new hairstyles on me, or stitch some nice shoulder bag. I used to borrow books for her from the library and whenever a new movie was released, she would take me along. I would enjoy her company. Banabhatta always commented, 'What is the use of reading novels? They will unnecessarily take you to imaginary worlds. It is better to read religious books, which will guide you on the way to *moksha* or heaven.'

For any social functions, Parvati and I were more frequent a pair than Banabhatta and Parvati. When I grew up, the frequency of my meetings with Parvati lessened. But, whenever I visited, she would ask, 'Nali, tell me one thing. What do you and your husband speak about?'

I thought that a strange question. 'What do you mean by that, Parakka?'

'I have never really had a conversation with my husband. I am simply curious.'

'Office work or a movie or a book.'

'Nali, there is nothing to hide from you. Everyone knows about our family. They make fun of our life. We have never sat together and spoken about a common interest. Banabhatta doesn't even know another life exists in his house.'

'Parakka, why don't you adopt a child?' I said with hesitation.

'I would love to, but Banabhatta doesn't want to. He says that if God has not given us children, then that is his wish. Let us not defy his wish.'

'Why can't you have some animal—perhaps a dog or a cat—in the house?'

'That is out of the question. Banabhatta doesn't allow a cat or a dog to come inside the house. As per the scriptures, he says.' Slowly, tears began rolling down her cheeks. For the first time, I realized how lonely Parvati was.

She went on. 'When my mother died, I was four years old. My father remarried and I had a stepmother. She never loved me. They didn't care about my education, and I studied only till class ten. I wanted to go to college, study hard and work later, but I wasn't allowed. I wanted to impress my stepmother and used to do good housekeeping and cooking, but she never appreciated my work. It was like pouring water on a boulder. She never changed.

'Then one day my father told me that my marriage has been fixed to a man I had never met. I saw the groom only at the wedding. There was a ten-year age difference between us, but my father's calculations were based on different factors. The groom had much gold and silver in his big house. His only sister was already married. There were no parents, so no one to trouble me. That was his criteria and he never asked what mine was.

'After marriage, of course, I became queen of the house but was never loved by my husband. I have always dreamt of having a loving and caring husband with whom I could share my entire life—a husband from whom I can get so much love that I could drown myself in it. I am so thirsty for love but my life has been like that of a traveller in a desert searching for water.'

'Parakka, why can't you go and talk to him?'

'I have tried but his answers are monosyllabic.'

'Is he upset because you don't have children? Perhaps you should visit a doctor. Am I crossing the line?'

'No, Nali, not at all. You are the only one with whom I am so open because you are not like the others. I tried to tell him many times what I wanted, about how we should be, but he doesn't listen. At the time of my wedding, everybody envied me—"Look at Paru, how many ornaments she has," they said. They never realized that ornaments cannot substitute for happiness. Your grandmother has always said that I am the best at many things but not even once has such praise come from him.'

'You are so intelligent, Parakka,' I said. 'Why do you want your husband to praise you? Everybody else praises you. Isn't that good enough?'

'Maybe I am wrong but as a wife, I expect certain things from him. The very purpose of marriage is to share, praise, lead and uplift each other. Do these things not figure in the vows we take before the sacred fire?'

'But it is not about you, Parakka. He is like this with everyone. He doesn't talk to people at all.'

'There is nothing wrong in his nature, but such people should not marry people like me. I wish I could change myself, but I can't.'

I had no answer. Banabhatta thinks differently, I thought. For him, women should be at home, performing pujas and chores. There is nothing really to talk with them about unless there is an emergency. Women can talk with other women and men can talk with other men. However, these are two parallel lines that never intersect.

*

The other day I received a call from my mother. With a heavy voice, she said, 'Your friend Parvati died of a heart attack this morning. I am going to her house with Janaki.'

My Parakka had just died. I remembered her in many forms. The bright bride who came to our town. The beautiful Parvati who came to our house. The affectionate

Parvati who cooked for me. The romantic Parvati who told me that she wanted to drown in love. Was this Parvati reduced to a handful of ash? Had this Parvati disappeared in the blue sky? I just could not imagine! My tears flowed uncontrollably.

At the end of the day, my mother filled me in on what had transpired.

Parvati had had a bath in the morning and was reading a book. She just passed away on the couch.

When they went to see her, she was her usual neat self, wearing a crisp Coimbatore cotton sari, with a half-moon bindi on her forehead and jasmine flowers in her hair. The green bangles in her hand looked bright as if they had been bought just yesterday. It just looked as if she was asleep, her sari fluttering gently under the fan.

Once again, the tears poured from my eyes for Parvati. I thought of calling up Banabhatta the next day and wondered what I should say.

'O Banabhatta, you lost a great woman.' Or 'O Banabhatta, why didn't you care for your wife?' Or 'O Banabhatta, it is God's wish.'

As I was preparing to call him, the phone rang. It was my mother. She said, 'Banabhatta died today. I have to go with Janaki again.'

'Don't keep the phone down yet. I want to know. How did he die?'

'I don't know the details, but Bindu says that he was meditating and collapsed. I have a lot of work to handle.' She put the phone down.

I wondered, why had Banabhatta died within twenty-four hours of Parakka's death? Maybe he loved her so much that he could not bear to live his life without her. He might not have been able to express his feelings, but he was surely filled with an ocean of love for her and he had drowned in it without even knowing about it. In real life, they were never together. They never ate, went out or talked together, but they embarked on their final journey together. They were not made for each other from the world's viewpoint, but they were connected intrinsically to each other. What a way to go for a couple who truly loved each other without even telling the other about it.

7

Selfish Suman

Selfish was Suman's surname. She was brought up in an atmosphere of greed. Her mother Meera was selfish. Suman's father Venkatesh was even more selfish. Constantly under the influence of this combination, Suman became exponentially selfish. There was nobody in her house to tell her that it was wrong.

Suman's father was a Public Works Department engineer, and her mother was from a well-off family. Meera was fond of gold, so she could be seen more often in jewellery shops than in her home.

Once, Bindu took us children, including Suman, to Hampi, the capital of the Vijayanagara Empire. There, Bindu started with one of his usual lectures. All of us got lost in the sixteenth century as he described a bygone era. We were imagining the dancers, poets, queens, mistresses, horses, processions and the golden throne of Krishna Deva Raya.

During the time of our visit, Hampi was not crowded. We stayed near the monuments. We travelled with small bags that we kept nearby on the ground.

Suddenly, there was rain, but Bindu did not stop. He said, 'This rain will stop in a few minutes. Let us not stop the *Dussehra* procession. The show must go on.'

The rain did stop but when we got down, we realized that our bags were drenched, except Suman's. She had quietly got down when the rain had started, taken her bag and put it in a safe place. It was like she would concentrate on only one point. In this case, it was Sumi's self interest, her own bag and nothing else.

Bindu was extremely upset, 'Sumi,' he said, 'you could have saved everyone's bag. You should not have taken only yours.

'Sumi, the Vijayanagara Empire fell because of selfishness. Such things happen when people think of their advantage, rather than the greater good. A good leader should have a large vision and a larger heart.'

Though her selfish nature would hurt others, Suman never intended it to do so. According to her, she was following Arjuna's *Lakshyabhedi* (eye on the bird theory). In a context, it asks the readers to look for what is advantageous to them, live for self and to consider the self as the centre of life. Likewise, Suman would not think of anyone else.

Bindu didn't like this quality of hers at all. 'Of course, Suman is good-looking, but she can't spend all her time in front of the mirror. She should learn from history. Beautiful queens were never famous; on the contrary, their large-hearted counterparts were always remembered. She needs to first learn better Kannada,' Bindu ranted.

Hema, a benevolent person, also didn't like her much. She said that Suman was too engrossed in herself. The other day, Suman and Hema were travelling by bus. They saw a pregnant woman standing. Hema said, 'Suman, will you vacate your seat for her? You are young and you can stand.'

'What did she say, Hema aunty?' I asked her.

'Nali, she said, "Even the pregnant lady is young. If she wanted a seat she should have come early." And she did not get up. Ultimately, I got up.'

The other day Bindu and I were going to Dharwad. I saw Suman at the bus stop.

Bindu said, 'Nali, don't look that side. Sumi is standing there.'

I ignored him and stopped near Sumi. I asked, 'Are you coming to Dharwad?'

She asked, 'When are you planning to return?

'Today, 5 p.m.'

'From where?'

'From the university.'

She agreed and got into the car.

She adjusted her timetable in her mind and said, 'Okay, can you pick me up from the station when you are returning?'

Then I remembered, 'Sumi, my mom told me to buy some vegetables. I don't think I will be able to do that. Will you buy them for me? I will pay for them.'

'That is not a problem'. While returning, she did get the vegetables but while getting down at her house, she said, 'What about the money? The vegetables cost twenty rupees.'

'Sumi, if you would have gone by bus or train it would have cost more than twenty rupees. In fact, you should return the money to Nali,' Bindu said.

With great difficulty, I stopped Bindu and paid the money to Suman.

Suman didn't feel the way Bindu felt. She got her money back—that was her only aim.

Once, Bindu was telling us about Prince Siddhartha who later became the Buddha. Bindu described how he left his wife Yasodhara and their son Rahul and became a monk, after seeing an old man, a dead person, a person with a disease and a homeless person. Then, he asked a question, 'Do you think what Siddhartha did was right or wrong?'

'He must have been an extremely sensitive person,' I said. 'Because we see the same incidents, but we don't react like that,' I replied.

'O Nali! Fantastic! After all, you are Krishnakka's granddaughter. You think in the same way.'

'Bindu, you always give her all the credit. If I do well, the credit is given to her. If I don't, then you say, "Being Krishnakka's granddaughter, how can you do such a thing?"' I protested.

He laughed. Suman gave a different answer, 'Bindu, I consider Siddhartha to be foolish. He had everything. He was good-looking, had money, a beautiful wife and a young son. Whatever he wanted was at his disposal. He saw an old man. For that, why should he leave his family, go to a forest and meditate? What did he gain personally? Nothing.'

Bindu lost his temper for the first time, 'Suman, you prove that there is mud in your brain. What work Siddhartha did is great. The prince would have died anonymously like many others of his stature, but he became the Buddha, a man of compassion and established *Bodh Dharma*. If you go to any country, like Japan, China, Sri Lanka, Cambodia, Thailand or Myanmar, you can witness the expanse of Buddhism. By sacrificing his pleasures, he made a great impact on humankind.'

Even Yasodhara wouldn't have been as upset with Siddhartha as Bindu was with Suman.

Suman was unperturbed. All her activities were within the circumference of me, myself and mine.

Suman grew into a beautiful woman, but her nature did not change. Janaki used to say, 'Don't suggest a groom for her. We will get a bad name in the end.'

Suman had a friend named Shyamala. She was from an affluent family. However, she had ordinary looks. One Thursday, a prospective groom's party was supposed to see Shyamala. All our friends' mothers gave a warning, 'Don't go to Shyamala's house for any reason. There may be a misunderstanding. It has happened many times before.'

We understood their meaning and did not step out that day.

Suman also knew about the prospective groom's visit. But neither did her mother give her any warning, nor would she have bothered to listen anyway. That day, Suman dressed up well and went to Shyamala's house exactly when the boy was supposed to come.

'Shyamala, shall we go to the temple today?' she asked.

The moment Shyamala saw her, she knew what Suman was up to. The boy was happy to see the beautiful Suman. In a small town such as ours, the news spread quickly. The groom, Dr Ganesh, liked Suman over Shyamala and their marriage was fixed without any problem. Banabhatta was the priest. He said that the horoscopes matched.

Dr Ganesh was enchanted by Suman. Her parents were extremely happy. They had got a good boy without searching for one.

However, her true colours started showing after the wedding.

Ganesh was a good and helpful man by nature. Suman could not stand some of his habits. 'Why do you have to see patients for free in the evening? What do you gain from that? Why do you have to work on a Sunday in the orphanage?'

Thus, a difference of opinion crept into their marriage. Suman and Ganesh became the north and south poles.

She began showing her true colours in front of her mother-in-law too. She would ask for a good sari for some occasion and never return it. But she would not lend her saris to anyone.

If she accidentally stained or damaged the borrowed saris, she would cleverly fold it in such a way that her mother-in-law wouldn't be able to notice. Afterwards, she would say, 'I do not know what happened.' The mother-in-law realized what was happening and stopped giving her saris eventually. A passive war between them began.

Her mother-in-law had blood pressure and sugar problems. The moment she was a little unwell, Suman would pack up her bags and leave for her parents' home.

Ganesh would say, 'Don't go right now. Mum is unwell.'

But Suman would come up with numerous reasons.

'My body is aching.'

'My head is spinning.'

'My back is unbearable.'

'My stomach hurts too.'

Although he was a doctor, Ganesh could not diagnose his wife's ailments. She would not take the prescribed medicine and instead say, 'It is not improving.' He would let her go upon realizing what she was up to.

Suman would stay in her parents' home till her mother-in-law recovered. Her mother, Meera, once advised her, 'Sumi, stay in a joint family as long as you have the advantage. You can save money, and children can be looked after when you are not around. When someone is sick, inform me. I will send word to you saying that I am unwell, too, and so you can come here. Whenever you want to separate, always blame your mother-in-law. Nobody will help you other than you yourself. Have you not heard it mentioned in the Bhagavad Gita?' I think Suman's mother Meera has never understood the real meaning of the Gita.

'In the Gita, Sri Krishna says, who is your best friend— you, yourself.'

'Who is the worst enemy—you, yourself.'

Meera doesn't know the real meaning, so she had taught herself to be selfish, which Krishna never intended.

With this training, Suman became much more confident to play the next game.

We had a domestic help in our house named Chandra. She had come to us from the village, and we looked after her like our daughter. We knew her father. One day, Suman came to our house for a casual visit. She was worried. 'My mother-in-law wants to go to Badri on a pilgrimage and wants to stay with her daughter en route. She will be out for six months. I will have a lot of work.'

Janaki, who was sitting there, said, 'If I were her mother-in-law, I would not return at all.'

'Why can't you hire a girl like our help, Chandra? If you want, I can speak and find a girl for you.'

'But everyone cannot be like Chandra. If I trained someone to be like her, it would take at least six months and by then my mother-in-law will have returned. Then I won't need any help.'

Bindu interrupted, 'That means your mother-in-law is equal to a domestic help?'

Suman did not bother to respond to the comment. 'I know the solution. You send Chandra to my house right now. I will send her back after six months.'

'Sumi, I can't do that. We promised her father that she will stay with us. Can you not see the difficulties in our home—a bedridden grandmother, the birth of a child?'

Sumi shrugged. 'Oh, you will manage. You are efficient.'

I was surprised by her bluntness. Sumi looked at me, and said, 'Don't worry about Chandra's salary. I will pay her as much as you do.'

With courage, I said, 'That is not possible Suman.'

'Why?'

'Because I have worked very hard to get good help.'

Suman was very upset. She told everyone, 'Nali did not help me when I was in difficulty. She looked after only her family.'

I did not get upset with her as I was aware of her nature. The other day, I saw her in a sari shop but remembered Bindu's advice and ignored her.

However, she came up to me without hesitating as soon as she saw me. She asked, 'What are you buying?' She looked at the sari I was holding, and said, 'This sari is very beautiful.'

I knew what was to come next. 'Sumi, I placed the order in January. I got it in August. This is a black hand-embroidered sari that was first handwoven and then embroidered.'

'But I really love it. I have been searching for something like this for two months. Anyway, you know the shopkeeper.

Why don't you order another one for yourself? I will buy this one. How much does it cost? Tomorrow is my birthday. I wanted to buy something special for myself.'

Before I could say anything, the salesman replied, 'Ma'am I won't sell the sari to you. This has been booked by this ma'am. If you want, I can book another order now and you can pick it up after six months.'

He closed the packet and gave it to me.

Suman said, 'I will now be disappointed on my birthday. I couldn't buy what I wanted to buy.'

*

Suman's husband got transferred to a village. By then, Suman had a son and wanted to keep him in the town. Her parents too stayed there, near the child's school. But they did not offer to keep their grandson. Ganesh requested them, 'It is only for a year. I will come back. It is a promotion transfer, and I cannot say no.'

Meera said to herself, 'Only two of us are there. We can go on holiday somewhere. We are bound to stay home if there is a school-going child around.' Though he was their grandson, she gave ten reasons why she couldn't keep the child.

'These days I am not well and have to go to the doctor regularly. We are retired people. We sleep early.'

She told her daughter, 'It is better your husband's sister can keep the child. Your husband has helped them a lot. Don't give anything for free. Take advantage of the situation.'

Ganesh knew what was going on in the minds of the mother and daughter. He was hesitant to ask his sister because the school was away from her house and she did not live in a joint family, who could help when needed. But still, his compassionate sister kept Ganesh's son with her.

Meera said, 'Beta, we are close by. Whenever you have time, please come for some time to see us.' And she closed the matter.

After six months, Ganesh's brother-in-law fell ill and was admitted to the hospital. His sister called Suman and said, 'Please come back and stay with your son till my husband comes back from the hospital.'

'I wish I could, but I have already booked my tickets to Ooty, where I am going with friends. After I return, I will definitely come then.'

Ganesh's sister lost her patience, and said, 'In that case, please take your child back.'

'I can't do that either. It is the middle of the term,' said Suman and put the phone down.

At last, Ganesh felt sorry for his sister and took leave from work to help her. He apologized to her. 'It was an unfortunate moment when I fell for her beauty. I should have checked what her mother was like. I hope the selfishness does not transmit to our child.'

Suman, without any worry, went on her trip.

Legend says Savitri went behind Yama, the lord of death, to beg for her husband's life. Yama lured her with money, kingdom and everything, but she didn't take it. She asked, 'Let my father-in-law get the kingdom, my father should have an heir, but ultimately, my husband must live.'

Today, in the same land we have a Suman who stands for selfishness and only looks out for her advantage in any situation. Even a blooming tree gives flowers, shade, fruit and a place for the birds, and at last, is burned at the funeral pyre. Never can our Suman understand that.

8

Adventurous Bhagirathi

Bhagirathi was brought up in a joint family that had lots of uncles and aunts. As a young girl, she was free of responsibilities. She would spend her time climbing trees, playing with her boy cousins and going with them to the fields for joy.

When she completed her class tenth, she expressed her desire to become a schoolteacher. She was interested in reading mythology and poetry. But as per the norms of society during those days, she was married when she was eighteen.

She entered another joint family, entirely different from hers. Her husband, Ramchandra, was educated and extremely pious but timid. He had four unmarried sisters and a widowed mother who was like a simple cow. Her husband's uncle, Shripad, and his wife oversaw the house—

they noticed all the activities. The family lived in a large house, perched on land that spanned hundreds of acres.

Smart Bhagirathi realized in no time that even though she and her husband were the owners of half the property, they were treated like good-for-nothings. They were only made to work and were at the mercy of their uncle for their income.

She thought over it and asked her husband and mother-in-law, 'How about dividing the property?'

They were taken aback. 'How can you talk like that? What will uncle think?' they retorted.

Bhagirathi said calmly, 'You have a lot of responsibility. Your sisters have to be married and it requires money. We have to divide it one day or the other. Haven't you heard of the famous saying? *"Haveli ki umr saath saal* [A haveli lasts up to sixty years]." No joint family will live together for more than sixty years. Whereas, you have lived together much longer than that.'

When uncle heard this proposition, he got upset. Finally, after a lot of tussles, he said, 'Fine. We will give you a house on the outskirts of the city, five hundred rupees and the grains required for your family, once a year.'

Ramchandra accepted the deal and came back to his house.

The house was far away from the town and possessed a scary demeanour. There were no neighbours. Ramchandra's family cursed Bhagirathi for the deal.

A year passed. Bhagirathi realized that this kind of dependency on her husband's uncle would not help. Thus, she asked him for land.

The uncle got upset. 'You are the one who has manipulated my nephew. Otherwise, he would not have asked for a share in the land. Though we have many acres, we don't grow much. We farmers depend on rain. He is just like my son. I might have given him more. Bhagirathi, in our family, no woman comes with the intent to divide the property. You please stay away.'

Bhagirathi realized that this was a do-or-die situation. If she left now, this would continue forever and her weak husband would keep on accepting whatever his uncle would say. So, she said, 'No. We want our land. I will come after a few months. You must make a fair division by then.'

As vowed, she returned for it while pregnant. Uncle said, 'I am not giving you the land. Do whatever you want. Do you want to go to court? Then go.'

Bhagirathi's asset was the balance of her mind. Without getting upset she said, 'Yes, I will go to court.'

When she returned home, her mother-in-law and husband were upset. 'You have brought a bad name to the family. In our family, no woman has gone to court. At least he was giving us some grains and money, now he will stop that also. Where is the money to go to court? It will take many years.'

Bhagirathi did not lose hope. 'Okay, I will not ask you for money. My parents gave me gold when I got married. I will sell or mortgage as much as I need. I am going to have a baby. Our family has to survive on its own, one way or the other.'

She approached her cousin Raghavendra, who was a lawyer.

'Raghu, tell me, what are my chances of winning? I don't know the law. If there is a slim chance of our victory, then I have to make alternate arrangements. Tell me as a brother. I can't pay your fees now, but if I win, I will pay it later in some form. That much I can assure you. Please help me.'

Raghu saw the case and said, 'Bhagi, don't worry. You will get your share, but it will take some time, and you must be patient to wait.'

Bhagirathi mortgaged her jewellery and gave the initial money required to start the case. Then she began working in a field near her home. The court case remained open all that while.

Uncle Shripad hired a big lawyer and spent more money. The case dragged on for three or four years. After the experience, Bhagirathi has always advised, 'You shouldn't go to court, avoid it as much as you can. Because the man who wins loses a lot of money. The one who loses is a dead person. It is not an easy war. But if it is inevitable, then you must.'

Those three or four years were very tough for her. She had her second child during that span.

Finally, uncle Shripad lost the case, and a hundred acres of land was allocated to her. Now everybody praised her. Bhagirathi paid Raghu's fees four times over.

Now, Bhagirathi had to take care of the hundred acres. She knew her husband could not help much. She would get up at 5 a.m. to cook and at 7 a.m., she would take farmer

Siddu with her, hire coolies and start working. She told me, 'Nalini, I understand farming. I learnt it with my cousins in the village for fun. But when it comes to real life, I have to think practically about what will be useful. I need to learn every aspect—seeding, cleaning, crop-cutting. I am also ready to work as a coolie in their absence. It is not difficult, but it does require strong common sense. You are playing with the Gods of sun, rain and wind, and along with that, you require people and animals to help you. I realize that.'

To be a successful farmer, you need to be able to motivate the people who work with you. What they teach in Indian Institutes of Management today, Bhagirathi has learned through her common sense. She applied it to real life and even today, not a single farmer or coolie has quit working for her unceremoniously. She opened bank accounts for all the farmers, took care of their food, gave them grains from the harvest along with money—she considered them family. Her theory was very simple: we are farmers. If we sow ten grains, we get a thousand grains in return. We do not do much. It is nature that gives us her bounty. So, we have to share the crop with our people. We should not selfishly say that every grain is mine and that we should sell to make money.

The crop was bumper as the management was super.

*

Uncle Shripad did not keep quiet. He would throw stones at Bhagirathi's lonely house on the outskirts of the city. He sent thieves to cut the crops. When the groom's party came to see her sister-in-law, he indulged in rumour mongering. When she stored dry hay for the cows, he hired goons to burn it. He got involved in many activities other than looking after his own farms.

Yet, Bhagirathi didn't get upset.

She asked for a gun licence and got four hunter-dogs to look after the farm. In a place like our town, a woman asking for a gun licence invoked fear among everyone. They thought Bhagirathi was capable of anything and would even resort to killing. The dogs were very loyal to her and always protected the house.

Years passed.

Ramchandra's sisters got married to boys from good families. The sisters harboured a respect for Bhagirathi, and she took her place as their late mother. Whenever they had difficulties, she always helped them.

Uncle Shripad became softer by the day. Old age arrived with many diseases. His children didn't do well, whereas Bhagirathi's son Suresh studied hard and became a doctor. Suresh was aware of how uncle Shripad had troubled his parents and how his mother had worked hard and taken responsibility.

One day, uncle Shripad came to their house with a limp. Both Bhagairathi and Suresh saw him as he entered. Bhagirathi remembered how he had ill-treated her as a young girl and the hardships she had faced—from going to court to selling her ornaments, from dealing with stone-throwing on their home to the burning of her hay.

But she looked at Suresh with a determined mind, and told her son, 'A patient has come. You are a doctor. Do your duty. Don't charge him. He is an old, handicapped man.' Then she went inside.

No comments or remarks could hurt her this time. She was above all of it.

Ramchandra remained a mute spectator of this life drama. He spent most of his time in the Chinmaya Mission, helping orphans and attending philosophy conferences.

Some people had observed his attitude. They would say things like, 'Look at Ramchandra! So pious and detached from life. Look at Bhagirathi—always immersed in fertilizers, ploughing, making ponds and planting seeds.'

Bhagirathi did not take such comments to heart. She said to herself, 'If both of us went into social work, we would have landed up without land or money. To do good social work, you also require a strong economic background.'

Suresh became a desirable groom, and many women sent him proposals.

Bhagirathi was very keen to have a daughter-in-law, who had seen the difficulties of life.

One day, one of her distant relatives was getting married. Suresh and his parents went to the wedding.

The bride, Vasudha, was a good-looking and good-natured schoolteacher but came from a very poor family. She had another disadvantage. Her *nakshatra* (the auspicious birth constellation) was *Ashlesh*. She had been advised to marry a boy who doesn't have a mother. Her father searched a lot and at last, they had found such a boy. The boy was no match for this smart girl.

They were related to Janaki, who only heaped praises. 'What a match. A mixture of pepper and rice.'

'How did Vasudha agree to this?' wondered Ganga.

Even a person like Bindu felt like it was unfair. He slowly said to Bhagirathi, 'Even in the history of India marriages like this have only taken place with kings. Not with ordinary folk.'

A day before the wedding, the boy's aunt picked up a small fight during one of the rituals. 'We wanted Bedekar pickle, but you have given us a homemade one,' she said, 'The garland does not have a great smell. The suit that you have stitched for the boy is not very expensive.'

Vasudha was unhappy with the developments. Initially, she stopped short of crying. However, she was unable to hold her tears back for long.

The next morning was the *muhurta*, the auspicious time for the wedding. The groom's father demanded a big dowry and threatened to cancel the wedding, if they would not give it.

Bindu said, 'This is unfair. You are raising this demand at the time of the muhurta, knowing very well about the financial condition of the bride's family. This is not our culture.'

Nobody cared about what Bindu said.

Bhagirathi came forward, 'Bindu is right. The times have changed. Seeking or offering dowry is a crime.'

But the groom's aunt and the father did not agree to this. They said, 'Anyway she has a bad star. Maybe this is a sign, and we should not go ahead with the wedding.'

Within a half hour, the wedding was wrapped dramatically.

Bhagirathi went out of her way to beg the boy's father, 'Please. Have a large heart. Don't stop the wedding.'

'Bhagirathi, it is easy to talk. We are traditional people. We cannot agree to such things.'

'Please think about the girl. It may be hard to get a boy for her later.'

'If you are so worried, why don't you take her as your daughter-in-law? If you are so modern, let us see that now,' challenged the groom's father.

The entire *mandap* fell silent, including Bhagirathi.

'Bhagirathi, it is easy to talk about things, but difficult to execute them. You can always advise somebody else's son. Can you do that for your own son?' asked the boy's father.

She did not answer. She took her son and husband aside into a room.

People gossiped outside. 'How can Bhagirathi marry this girl to her son? The girl is so poor and has a bad star. She has come for the wedding. If it doesn't happen it is not her problem. Why should she go out of her way?'

Inside, Bhagirathi looked at her son. 'Suresh, do you like the girl? We know her family.'

Suresh read his mother's mind. He was surprised. 'But Amma . . .'

'Don't worry. If you like the girl, we will go ahead. I don't believe I will die because of her star but if I do, it is still okay as I have completed my duties to my family and the farmers. I have not done any *janaseva* to society like your father. Whenever my end comes, I will be happy that I could give life to a girl.'

Ramchandra had tears in his eyes. He thought, 'What did my wife do all these years? She took the responsibility for our family. And now she is offering life to a girl. Is that not a great social service?' He did not say anything and just held her hand. Appreciation and love prevailed in that moment of silence.

The three of them came out of the room. Bhagirathi went straight to Vasudha, wiped her tears with her *pallu* and said, 'Here is my son. Do you like him? If so, tell me without hesitation. If not, then also tell me. If you do, you can marry my son in the same muhurta. We don't want any dowry and I don't care about what people say.'

And so, in this very filmy way, Suresh married Vasudha. The bride is now very happy in Bhagirathi's house. Whenever she lights a lamp, she always touches her mother-in-law's feet.

In the ensuing years, my town exploded into a city. Bhagirathi's 100 acres on the outskirts were absorbed into urban spaces. It became hard for her to continue cultivation amid rampant developments.

Suresh thought about it for a long time and said to his mother, 'Amma, we can't do farming now. How about turning this land into residential plots and selling them? I know it will hurt you tremendously. Think it over and tell me. I will do whatever you want.'

Bhagirathi did not talk or eat for two days. She had been with these farms for fifty years. They were her parents, teachers, God, food—everything. How could she live without this? This land had helped in difficult periods. It had stood by her as a loyal friend. How could she leave it? But she was also practical. She called Suresh, and said, 'I agree. Turn the land into residential plots but on one condition. You buy more land somewhere else. A farmer is always a farmer. Make plots but distribute some to the coolies who have been with us for a long time. Give your aunts also one plot each. I don't need anything.'

Suresh followed his mother's instructions. He knew her mind was convinced but her heart was not. He made a layout of the residential area and called it Bhagirathi Nagara.

All her coolies and helpers built their own houses, for which they were extremely grateful.

A few years later, Ramchandra suffered a stroke and was bedridden. Bhagirathi served her husband patiently, despite a nurse being around to help.

Though she was sad, she lightened up at my sight. 'Come Nali. Have you come to see your kaka?'

'Yes, how is he?'

She took me to Ramchandra's room. It smelled of medicine. Ramchandra could not even turn in his sleep without pain. It was hard for me to see this harmless, sincere man suffer. Without saying much, I came out.

Bhagirathi and I walked out and sat below a tree.

'Nali, I am just thinking out loud. But I pray to God to let me be a widow . . . to let your uncle go. I like him. I respect him. I cannot see him suffer this way. I always believed in his betterment, and it is his time to go. I don't want him to live for my selfish reasons.'

I always appreciated Bhagirathi's unbiased opinions. Her mind was consistently balanced.

I don't know whether she had this courage or balance from childhood, or it was something she developed over the years. Sometimes, I feel that a person like her should help the government or the nation. She would have made excellent decisions. In the small periphery of her family, she lived like a captain and steered all its members.

The next week, I got the news of kaka's passing. I reflected upon Bhagirathi aunty's sad face and her strong words.

9

Miser Jeevraj

A few days ago, my cousin Prakash visited from California. He had sold his dot com start-up and become a rich man within a few years. The conversion rates meant Prakash, also known as Pakya, could spend a lot of money in India. When we went to our village's Maruti temple, he gave two hundred rupees as *dakshina*. When the priest smiled looking at the donation, Pakya whispered in my ears, 'Nali, what is so great? It is less than three dollars.'

He organized a get-together, where he invited all of us cousins. He gave each of us ten thousand rupees and five thousand rupees to the elderly as a gift. He told us, 'These days, everything is available in India. Hence, I didn't bring any gifts. Please buy whatever you like.'

When he saw Jeevraj in the corner of the verandah, he asked me, 'Nali, who is that fellow?'

I had to explain how Jeevraj was related to us. Normally, people have family trees to show their members from different generations, but in our house, it was more of a family forest. Our many cousins, aunts and aunt's aunts made for perhaps the most complicated family tree of which Jeevraj was only one leaf.

Jeevraj was busy looking at the muted television, which was tuned into CNN. A programme was showing stock prices. Looking at his clothes, Pakya said, 'Nali . . . that poor man! Poverty is very bad and painful. Sometimes, it takes away your mind. But he is watching CNN even in his poverty. He may not have any money to invest, but desire and hope are great strengths. Do you think I should give him the same gift as the elderly quota?'

I started laughing. 'Pakya, who are you calling poor?'

He pointed to Jeevraj and said, 'That fellow.'

'Thank God, he didn't hear you. Pakya, he can probably buy you out.'

'What?' Prakash was surprised.

Jeevraj was dressed in the suit his father-in-law had gifted him at his wedding many years ago. It had faded and looked dirty and old. Thus, Prakash assumed that he was poor. But in reality, he was rich. The buffalo might be black, but the milk isn't. What you see on the outside is different from the inside.

Jeevraj had four commercial buildings in the town. He owned hundred-acre wetlands near the river Krishna. He had a safe at home. The locker might have looked extremely old with its worn-out paint but was filled with pure gold. Apart from that, he had a chit business and had invested in good shares.

Jeevaraj was known as *Lakshmi putra*, a rich man, but also as *Saraswati shatru*, not learned. He is one of the worst misers I have ever seen. In his vocabulary, there is always a plus and multiply. No minus or divide.

Jeevraj's conversations were very different from what would be considered normal. 'Nali, what's your salary?' he would ask without hesitation.

'Forty thousand rupees,' I replied with hesitation.

'What about your husband's?' he continued the investigation without any sensitivity.

'Around sixty thousand rupees.'

'Oh, now I know. That is a total of Rs 1 lakh. it means you collectively earn Rs 12 lakh in a year. In ten years, it will be Rs 1.20 crore.'

'Not like that Jeevraj. In one hundred years, she will earn Rs 120 crores,' Bundle Bindu immediately replied.

In our culture, even when people are wrong, we don't point it out to them. It is considered bad manners. So, I pulled on Bindu's shirt to shush him. But he didn't realize what I was doing.

'Don't pull my shirt, Nali. You are going to earn Rs 120 crores in the next hundred years,' he laughed.

Jeevraj did not laugh.

'What is wrong with that? Nali makes good money.' Bindu was persistent.

'Come on Jeevraj, be practical. Both of us earn money, but we also have expenditures. Food, clothing and others,' I said.

'Explain to me Nali, what does others mean? I am assuming food, clothing and stay take 10 per cent of the salary. You have your own house to stay in and fields. You get your grains from the agricultural produce.'

'Jeevraj, it's not like that. I have to spend time at my farm also. Then there are other things, like taking sick family members to the hospital, gifting on special occasions like Diwali, vacations, children's education, clothing and extra classes,' I kept explaining the expenditure.

'Come on, Nali. If you go on spending like this, even a salary of Rs 1 crore will not be sufficient. Why do you have to buy clothing every year? After all, clothes are perishable. Use it until they tear. And don't use a fantastic menu for your house—normal chapati, dal and vegetables. Control your expenditure by having a kitchen garden. It is good for your health also. A penny saved is a penny earned.'

It is very difficult to converse with such a man. In his dictionary, there must be no entertainment, no books—it is all a waste. I don't ever remember Jeevraj buying a new outfit for any festival. His idol was Gandhi.

'The real man is Gandhi. Look at him! He only had two pieces of clothing, which served many purposes. Once torn, they can be converted into a bedsheet or curtain and when further torn, a towel. Look at what he consumed—he ate groundnuts and drank milk. It is very good for your health.

If Godse had not killed him, he would have hit a century. Excess eating is not good, Nali. Learn from Gandhi.'

Jeevraj attended all the weddings in the town. The other day, I had seen him at Suvarna Desai's wedding.

'How do you know them? Did they call you?' I asked. Suvarna was my junior in college.

'Why should they give me an invitation, Nali?' Jeevraj said. 'Open that invitation in your hand—please come with your family and friends. Am I not in your family? So, I came.'

It was hard to teach etiquette to Jeevraj, who would land up at all weddings without an invitation.

He never gave a gift on any occasion to anyone. His philosophy was, 'Whatever a man receives as a gift has limitations and whatever God gives is for life. So, he doesn't give anything. He only gives blessings, "May God give you whatever you want."'

Then he would have a good meal and go back home. Though he preached to others about the importance of a simple diet, he ate like a *Bakasura* (a mythological giant with a huge appetite) at weddings.

Jeevraj's house was old and large. The verandah had a torn carpet, a three-legged unbalanced chair, which was supported by a stone. No whitewash had ever been done, and there was one photo of Goddess Lakshmi on one of the verandah walls. Inside, you would find Jeevraj sitting for lunch before an aluminium plate and a tumbler. He will eat at home when it was not the season for weddings.

His wife Manjula was tired of him after all their years of marriage. She doesn't say a word. She serves him food as if she was serving it to someone despicable.

Though Jeevraj is related to me, I liked Manjula aunty more and it is with her that I chatted frequently.

Once I asked her, 'Manjula aunty, how do you live with him?'

'I am in hell. At first, I felt like running away. Now I don't. I am used to this life. I pray to God that I do not pick up this miserly quality from my husband, so I say very little with him.'

'Manjula aunty, how did you end up marrying this fellow?'

'It was destiny. I was mad at that time. I did not have proper guidance, I suppose. When the proposal came, there were only two people in this house—Jeevraj and his mother. They came to our house and saw me. My father brainwashed me by saying, "Look, there are only two of them at home, so you won't have much work. They are very rich. Your mother-in-law is a nice lady. So, you can be a queen there." I was young and got carried away. Once I was married and came to this house, I was shocked. At that time, the house was just the same as it is today. Initially, I thought maybe there are no young people, so there had been no one to manage the home. But after I entered, I realized that this family had a different mindset. Buying anything is taboo in this house. It seems Jeevraj's father was like that. They gave me plenty of gold at the wedding, but one cotton sari. Your uncle told me, "Why waste money on a new sari? The same money I can give to chit funds and earn more."

'After the wedding rituals took place, he took back all the gold saying, "If you wear it regularly, it will lose its shine and wear out." He kept it in the locker, and I have worn it only once in all my life. Our richness is seeing money in the mirror. You can only see and enjoy. You can't take it . . . like a ladoo for a diabetic patient.'

Manjula aunty, being a nice lady, continued to live with him. He brought the rations every month so that his wife cannot prepare or eat more than the allotted amount. But her brothers and sisters were very generous, and she gets additional rations from them.

The other day, I saw Jeevraj in a readymade clothing store. I was shocked to an extent. How could Jeevraj be in a readymade store? I forgot where I was heading and entered the shop to satisfy my inquisitiveness.

He was arguing with the shopkeeper while purchasing a vest. 'This is not fair. The thirty-two-sized vest costs hundred rupees; the size thirty-four also costs the same and the size thirty-six too. There will be more cloth in thirty-six than thirty-two, right?'

Knowing Jeevraj, the shopkeeper said, 'I don't want to know your logic or argue with you, that too in the morning for my first sale. The label says hundred rupees. If you want to take it, please do, else don't spoil my day.'

This is a typical North Karnataka way of shopping. If you go to Gujarat, and enter a sari shop by mistake, the salesman will make you feel like you are a queen. '*Behenji,* please sit down. Madam, can I put the fan on? Or can I get some cold water, ma'am? Please see the saris. Just see.'

'Show me saris for five hundred rupees.'

'Don't worry. For five hundred rupees I will show you five hundred saris. You don't have to buy anything. God has given you eyes. Just see and feel happy.'

The more he showed, the more I bought—three saris.

Whereas the Hubli shopkeeper had turned away his face and spoke to the next customer.

Jeevraj saw me and told me the entire episode of the vests.

'How does it matter what the label is, Jeevraj? If the size is suitable for you, buy it.'

'Okay fine.'

And he bought size thirty-six, though he actually wanted thirty-two, just because there would be more cloth in that.

Once, all of us went to Canara Café in Hubli. On the way, I saw Jeevraj.

'Why don't you come?' I invited Jeevraj, though others were disapproving.

'Oh Nali, what is the reason?'

'I got an award, so I am giving you a simple treat.'

Jeevraj became very large-hearted, 'It should not be simple Nali. It should be great. You should have told me in the morning.'

'Yeah,' I thought. 'If I had told him in the morning, he would have fasted through lunch.'

We sat on the terrace and as soon as the server came to our table, Jeevraj started ordering, 'One gulab jamun, a bonda, upma, one dosa, idli.'

I stopped him, 'Don't read the menu. It is a simple party, and I will order.'

The server smiled and said, 'Neither of you order. Today is our tenth anniversary so we give everyone free coffee and Dharwad peda.'

Immediately, Jeevraj said, 'In that case, we are eight people. Get eight pedas.'

'There are only four of you,' said the server.

'Another four are about to come.'

'They will not get it if they are outside. Only people who sit here get the sweets,' said the server to our face, and went away.

We all felt embarrassed at his behaviour.

Some of us bet to make Jeevraj spend money one day. Bundle Bindu was a part of this challenge. I started pestering Jeevraj, 'You must take us for a movie.'

'What is there in the movie?'

He gave us a hundred reasons to not go. At the end, Manjula aunty intervened, and said, 'You call Nali for all the odd jobs, and she does them with a smile. She is only asking for a movie. If you can't agree, next time Nali will charge you,' she said, without consulting me.

'But you shouldn't come,' he said to reduce the charge of one ticket. 'Nali, let's go in an auto. Can you pay for it?'

While we were standing in the queue for the ticket, Bundle Bindu joined us. Seeing him, Jeevraj said, 'You have also come!'

'Because you are showing a movie. It is like the sun rising in the west. So, I thought I should come and celebrate.'

After a few minutes, when the tickets queue neared the counter, he said, 'I will come in a minute.'

He did not show up. By then our turn for movie tickets had arrived, and I couldn't locate Jeevraj anywhere.

At last, I bought three tickets. As soon as I left the window, Jeevraj came from nowhere.

I lost the bet and the ticket money, too.

He was not a bad person. He was neither the jealous kind nor was he a gossipmonger. He did not interfere with others' lives. He spent his energy saving his money. His reading habits were not so great. The last books he had read were his textbooks. Thus, his knowledge was limited, and his ideas were old-fashioned. His value system is based on money. He thinks having a daughter is very expensive. Having a son is an advantage.

He reasoned that a girl cannot give returns on the money spent on her. He would say that she goes on to earn money with her husband. When I tried to say that the son doesn't give returns either, he refused to acknowledge it. He said the money remains in the family.

He has a daughter, Mangala, and a son, Keshav. Fortunately, both of them have taken after their mother's nature—nice and large-hearted. They are quiet children. When Keshav came of age, Jeevraj took the charge of finding him a bride. He said, 'Nali, do you know a girl who is earning and comes from a rich family and is an only child?'

'Weddings can be simple,' he added. 'They can take place in a temple, and one need not invite the whole town.

They don't have to gift us any vessels, furniture etc. We have it all.'

In my mind, the three-legged chair and torn carpet flashed before my eyes. They can save all that money and put it in a fixed deposit.

'How should the girl be?' I asked.

'What is there? She should be normal. All girls look beautiful when they are young. After one or two children, they become fat. Colour and all don't matter.'

In his dictionary, there were no romantic notions about marriage.

'Jeevraj, we can ask Keshav what he likes in a girl?'

'What is there? He is an officer in a bank. I told him to take the cashier's post so he can have the joy of counting money. I am also searching for a groom for Mangala.'

The standards are the same except for the gender. That was the only difference.

But fate had different plans.

Keshav fell in love with his colleague Mamta, a Delhi girl with an army upbringing. Jeevraj did not accept this alliance. But when Mamta came and saw Keshav's home, she said, 'I cannot accept this proposal. Keshav, come and see my house, and how I was raised. We always had a huge bungalow, with a big friend circle. We believe in eating well and living a good life. We enjoy every day. I can't adjust to your parents' lifestyle.'

Jeevraj refused to go to Delhi because of the train fare, but Manjula aunty sent Keshav by air. She said, 'Don't listen to your father. Take a flight with your own money.

Meet the people. Marriage is not just between you two; you also have to adjust to their home. Don't worry about your father's consent. He will never say yes. And the type of girl he will choose, you will never marry.'

Jeevraj threatened his son, 'If you marry her, I will disown you and you will never get any inheritance from me.'

'Don't worry about your dad's money. Both of you are earning and you can manage on your own. Don't lead the shabby life that was forced upon me. Once you have children, your father will also change.' Saying this, Manjula pushed Keshav to marry Mamta.

A grand wedding took place in Delhi. It was our first trip to the national capital. Jeevraj came but did not speak to anyone. Keshav spent all his earnings, gave a new outfit to his father and took care of the airfare, the train charges and the bride's gifts. Fuming, Jeevraj did not give a gram of gold and Keshav took a transfer to Mumbai.

Defeated, Jeevraj now focused on searching for the right groom for Mangala. He had another disappointment in store. Mangala found herself her groom. Her college lecturer Muralidhar Rao wanted to marry her, and she also liked him. Manjula aunty was very happy. Muralidhar Rao was well-educated and from their own community.

Jeevraj asked the boy about the details of the Rao family.

'I don't have a father and have two sisters to be married off. I am doing my PhD and may get a promotion in time. I don't own a house or land. But I will keep your daughter happy.'

His mother also said the same. They were nice, simple people.

This time again there was a Mahabharata-like situation in the family. Manjula encouraged her daughter to go for this alliance. All her dreams were coming true through her children. Again, Jeevraj threatened to cut off ties with Mangala.

Mangala and Muralidhar got married in Tirupathi. As usual, Jeevraj attended the wedding as a mere guest. He did not give his daughter anything.

Manjula begged her husband to give her two bangles and a chain from the locker to wear for her daughter's wedding. Maybe after seeing Keshav's glamorous Delhi wedding, he gave those to her or maybe he wanted to show off his wealth to Rao's family.

At the time of the wedding, Manjula took two off her bangles and chain and gave them to Mangala. Jeevraj was shocked and unable to speak. By the time he could recover, the wedding got over.

For the next ten days, Jeevraj did not speak to his wife. She felt it was like a *vipassana* course. Jeevraj did not speak to his wife, but Manjula was too happy to bother about him.

This was the first time that all his calculations had gone wrong. Neither his son nor his daughter had valued his money enough to stay back. He had always thought that money gave him an edge and they would listen to him because of it. But today's generation was different. They cared for a balanced life, happiness, their partners and their partners' opinions, all of which Jeevraj had never heard of.

Muralidhar Rao soon received his PhD and was transferred to Bengaluru. Mangala got a job in a high school.

Due to his nature, Jeevaraj could never make any friends. Manjula aunty, though, always had a friend circle.

As time passed, Jeevraj became lonely. He thought deeply about where he went wrong but couldn't come up with an answer.

For the first time in his life, he began to receive invitations to weddings and other family occasions, addressed to him in person. However, he no longer cared for free food or entertainment and did not respond.

Unfortunately, he had a stroke. He had never been to a doctor for a checkup in his life.

Mangala being nearby, took him to Bengaluru and got him treated. Muralidhar did a lot for him during this time and never took a penny from him. Jeevraj was able to walk again with the help of a stick and soon returned home.

The other day I went to see him. He was elated. 'For my sake Nali, you have come all the way and even taken a day off?'

'Yes, Jeevraj, I have taken unpaid leave, spent on a train ticket and bus fare. So overall, I have spent five hundred rupees,' I joked.

'It doesn't matter even if it is twenty thousand rupees. It is worth meeting people in such times,' said Jeevaraj.

'What? You are talking like this? Where did the sun rise from today? Are you feeling all right?'

'Yes Nali, life has taught me some lessons, though I never learnt any despite many trying to teach me. Money is required in life, but it is not everything.'

'The way Mangala and Murali served me, I felt ashamed of how I used to think and speak about girls. Even though I want to give money, they are not taking it. They are not rich, but they are happy. Murali looks after her very well and makes her happy, which I could never do for my wife. Keshav also called me, but I don't want to go there. There is a difference between a daughter and a son. You have more freedom with your daughter, and it is a little more formal with your daughter-in-law. Now, I want to be happy with everyone. You must now have one daughter, who will support you in your old age without expectations.'

'Are you sure?' I was surprised.

'Yes,' he said, adding, 'I have called my lawyer and asked him to divide my money into four parts—one to my wife whom I never valued until now, one to Mangala, one to Keshav and one to build a girls' residential hostel.'

It was the first time that I had a glimpse of a changed Jeevraj. He had never uttered the word 'donation' in his entire life until that very moment.

In real life, even though Jeevraj had not cleared his graduation, in the twilight years, he had passed life's exam with flying colours and earned the highest degree.

10

Amba the Super Chef

Amba was not a professional cook. But if you wanted to meet her, you could only do so by going to her kitchen.

Bindu always looks at her and remembers a story. 'Long back, Chandrika was a beautiful princess who was kidnapped by a magician. To bring her back, a handsome prince fought with all his might but was unable to defeat the magician. Someone said, "It is no point fighting with this cunning magician. His life is in the parrot he keeps protected in a cage. If you kill the parrot, the magician will die too." Thus, Chandrika was saved after the prince killed the parrot.'

'I'm not able to understand this story Bindu,' I interrupted.

'Nali, I think you don't read much,' Bindu immediately retorted. 'However, I will tell you. Like the magician, whose life was in the parrot, your friend Ambika's life is in the gas stove. If it is off, she is uncomfortable.'

I laughed at the analogy. Though it wasn't the truth, it was very close to it indeed. Amba loved cooking as if her life depended on it. She was the queen of the kitchen. Vessels, vegetables, fruits, spices and grains were her subjects. She could command any of these ingredients to work for her as she put her ideas to the test and cooked various exquisite, delicious dishes.

Amba's husband Anand was a Kannada lecturer at a college and extremely absent-minded. He was always immersed in either poetry or prose. For him, eating was the last thing he would enjoy. He would always comment, 'Food is only to fill your stomach, to live. Without that, you can't survive. That is its place in one's life.'

On the other hand, Amba would say, 'God is a wonderful creator. See how he has kept the sour taste in tamarinds, tomatoes and lemons and the sweetness in beetroots and sugarcane. Look how the combination of sweet and sour can make a great dish. I always wonder who found out you can make rice from rice grain, you can make puri from wheat grain. It is not that we have to eat many dishes every day, but whatever we eat must be tasty. Without tasty food, what would life be?'

Once, Amba invited me, and said, 'I read there is a tea ceremony in Japan, and it is supposed to be very important.'

'Of course, Amba. Even I have read about it. It says if you serve tea in a clean cup and saucer and prepare it with affection, then you are the greatest host.'

'Yes, I agree. I believe that if you cook a simple lunch or dinner with affection and a happy mind, then people relish it. If you are not happy to have the guest but force yourself to cook, even with the best ingredients, even sudharas will be better.' Sudharas is a dish prepared with lemon and sugar syrup.

When Anand heard the word sudharas, he immediately interjected, 'O Amba, the great poet Sudhakar has written a great poem on the rainy season. I am sure if you read it, you would really enjoy it.'

'O, that reminds me,' Amba said. 'Yesterday, when it was raining, I made fantastic pepper rasam, which is good for health and complements this rainy weather well. Wait, I will go and get you a glass.'

'Please bring it for us also,' I said.

'No, I am not interested in rasam,' said her husband. 'I want you to read Kalidasa's *Ritu samhara* where he talks about the different seasons.

'That reminds me. Every season has a special dish, and you should eat it only in that season. For example, different types of buttermilk can be made in the summer and winter . . .'

'Just stop it, Amba. I am not interested. I want you to read poetry on Krishna and Sudama in *Shatpadi* [a kind of metre in Kannada poetry, where six words make a line]. You will forget the world.'

'Sudama makes me think of Sudama poha. There are thirteen types of poha—wet poha, dry poha, deep fried poha, dadpe poha, etc.'

'Amba, enough is enough. The more I talk, the more you and your friends speak in a different direction. At home, I have 3000 Kannada and Sanskrit books. Why can't you read for an hour every day? But you don't even step into the library. I got married to you because your father said you were a BA in Kannada. But now I know you majored in cooking.' Anand got upset, put on his coat and went to the college library.

Amba looked at me with a worried face and said, 'When I was getting married, my father said that I was majoring in Kannada, but that does not mean I loved the subject. Why should my husband get so upset? In every marriage, there are always such white lies.'

Amba felt very sad for a few minutes.

I said, 'Amba, don't listen to Anand. He is like that ever since he was a kid. He would always trouble my aunt and was mindless when it comes to food. My aunt had to always run behind him with a plate. So, forget about it.'

Amba forgot her husband's scolding and went into the kitchen. I followed her.

Amba used to love people, and we friends were fond of her. One reason was her extraordinary cooking, and another was her unconditional love and affection. She always told me, 'Nali, don't come home without informing me. If you tell me two days in advance, then I can make some special dish for you.'

'Amba, how many dishes do you know?'

'Don't tell my husband.' She showed me her notebooks. She had more than 450 recipes.

'Have you tried them all?'

'Of course! I only write them down after trying.'

'Amba, don't you get bored sitting all the time in the kitchen?'

'Do you get bored reading all the time? Does Bindu get bored teaching history all the time? My kitchen is my lab, and its ingredients are the chemicals. Ingredients come into my dreams, and say, "Amba, if you are intelligent, using us in different combinations will make for a different taste." The next day morning, I get up and make it. Do you know, using rice I can make as many as ten dishes, some savoury, some sweet—different types of pulaos and kheers?'

I was amazed at her experience.

Amba does not know the importance of time. The other day, one of my cousins, Prakash, came from America. He was Amba's classmate, so he came to visit her. When he reached her home, it was already 4 p.m. By then, he had already had tea, coffee, lemonade and other drinks and food everywhere else. It was probably the sixth house he was visiting that day. He was tired.

She was happy to see her classmate. 'O Pakya, how are you? When did you come? What can I make for you?'

'I am really tired of eating. I don't want anything. I only came to see you.'

'How can it be? I will make special lemonade at least.' Amba would not leave him.

'What kind of lemonade?' I asked.

'You want regular lemonade, mango lemonade, passion fruit lemonade or orange lemonade?' she said as if reading from a dictionary of lemonades.

Pakya didn't understand. 'Do whatever you feel like.'

He sat with us and Anand. After half an hour, she made three kinds of lemonade along with some dishes. As it was summer, she was sweating.

Prakash drank half a teaspoon of one lemonade, and said, 'It is getting late Amba. I have to go home now.'

He said his goodbyes and went away.

Amba was sad. 'Look at Prakash! I made so many nice things and he didn't even taste them or talk to me. I really wanted to know what the kitchens are like in the US, but he simply went away.'

Amba was annoyed.

'Ambu, that is your fault,' said Anand. 'If someone comes to meet us, they don't necessarily come to eat. People come to our house to meet and talk to us or share their ideas. As a host, you should offer some food but not keep insisting. He has to eat a little in all the houses that he visits and probably Prakash would have a stomach upset today, so he might not have eaten.'

Amba never understood it. Still, she felt that Prakash should have tasted the savoury dish that she had made in an unusual way.

In our friend circle, everyone asks Amba to share rare dishes. She does it voluntarily, charges no money and the food is of lip-smacking quality.

If in anyone's house, a prospective groom and his family had come to meet the bride and her family, Amba would brim with enthusiasm. The other day, the mothers of Vibha and Prabha told her to send mango barfi and khaman dhokla. But something else happened that day.

This is what Amba told me.

'I never knew that Vibha's mother and Prabha's mother don't talk to each other. Both called and said, "Please do this." I made the same dishes and sent it to their houses. The boy who visited Prabha's house ate mango barfi and khaman dhokla. Prabha's mom said, "This is made by Prabha. She is very good at cooking." Then he asked for more.

'The same evening, the boy went to see Vibha. There, the same dishes were presented, and he was told that Vibha has made them as she loves cooking. The lie was out in the open.

'I knew that Prabha and Vibha never go to the kitchen. They spent most of their time chatting or watching movies or on the phone.'

'Then what happened?'

'The prospective groom was smart. He said neither of these girls had cooked it, since the taste of the two dishes was identical. So, it was highly likely that it was cooked by a third person. Somehow, he got my address, and he called me.'

'Why did he call you, Amba? You are already married.'

'Come on, Nalini. This is for a different reason. He said, "Ma'am, your cooking is really great. I am extremely fond of eating. Do you have anyone in your family who cooks like you and who is looking to get married?"'

'What did you say, Amba?'

'I was taken aback. I didn't know that my cooking could alter someone's fortune. Then I remembered my uncle's daughter was of marriageable age and told him that. But I also told him I didn't know about her cooking skills.'

'Why did he want a girl who cooks?'

'He lives in a village in New Zealand. There are hardly any Indians and no Indian restaurants. He has to cook every day and eat by himself. He loves cooking and eating and wanted a companion who enjoyed it too.'

'What happened next?'

'He liked my cousin, Vanita, and said that he would come back after six months. For six months, he asked that Vanita come to my house and take lessons from me, and I should certify her cooking.'

'Did Vanita agree to go live in New Zealand? I wouldn't have,' I said.

'Of course, she did. There are no in-laws, no guests . . . just the husband and wife, who will be attached to each other. Now every day, she comes with a notebook to learn good cooking. I will tell Anand. He always pokes fun at my zest for cooking. But my cooking has changed Vanita's destiny.'

Amba not only cooked well but she was also quick. The other day, at my friend Soudhamini's house, there was a birthday party. She called all her friends; there were almost seventy-five people. The well-known cook Krishna was called that day and the menu included laddoo, upma, raita and sandwiches. However, Krishna fell that morning and broke his right hand. Soudhamini started crying as if she was the one who had been injured after taking a fall. It was wedding season and she knew she wouldn't get another cook.

She couldn't order from a hotel either because she had organized the party at her farmhouse, and it was difficult to reach.

In our small town, any such news spreads faster than the Internet. When Amba learnt of it, she went to Soudhamini's house.

'Soudhamini, am I your friend or not? I will do the main cooking, but I need two people to help. You don't worry. Call Nali. Though she may not help in cooking, she is good at serving and talking.'

'Amba, you are my friend and not a cook. Nali is also a friend. How can I tell her to serve?'

'Come on, Soudhamini. Are we not part of a big family? Don't you remember that whenever there was a big party in college, we all worked together in the kitchen? Let us share the load.'

Bindu said, 'In North Karnataka, people are more emotional and less practical. So, people go uninvited to offer help without expectations.'

We started the preparations under Amba's leadership. Amba concentrated only on cooking. She was faster than sprinter P.T. Usha was at the relay. Cutting and boiling vegetables, frying and grinding . . . all happened in a jiffy. She was multi-tasking and focused. I was the poor assistant who could not match her in handing her vegetables or serving food. She made more than what was on the menu. There were different lemonades, two types of laddoos, special upma, vegetable upma, crisp sandwiches. Everyone said Amba is like our Goddess Annapoorna.

Jayant also came to the party. He thought of himself as a practical person even though he isn't. 'Amba, you are such a fantastic cook. Why can't you open a cooking class? Lots of people may enrol, at least girls of marriageable age. Fix a fee of hundred rupees. Take my idea. You will be very successful.'

Janaki smiled and said, 'A wrong idea for a right person.'

After a few weeks, her 'Annapoorna' cooking class was opened. Ten people enrolled for the first batch. Some were married, and some weren't. Amba fixed the menu for each day. However, nobody liked it.

Nirmala said, 'Amba, teach us eggless cake. My mother-in-law is fond of it. She is upset with me for no reason these days, and I want to make her happy.'

'Our children are tired of eating my food and want to eat the north Indian variety. My husband is upset that I don't know north-Indian cooking. So, teach me that,' said Radhika.

'My husband is extremely fond of authentic sweets. I can't even recall the names. It seems my mother-in-law was a great cook. And she died. So, there is no guidance for me. It seems there is appli kheer, batwee kheer, dal kheer etc. I have to learn as my husband insists,' said Pramila with tears in her eyes.

I don't know how Amba managed to cater to the different menus of all these women.

Within a month, Amba's cooking class closed. Her cooking class followed the trajectory of Jayant's store.

One day I met Anand on the street. 'How is Amba's cooking class?' I asked.

'It is closed, and I had to spend five thousand rupees from my pocket,' said Anand angrily.

'Why?'

'Amba doesn't have any discipline. She went on teaching what they wanted, and she prepared a lot for everyone. The quantity of each dish that was prepared would suffice for all students. Thus, she ran a grocery bill of fifteen thousand while she earned ten thousand from their fees.'

I went to Amba's house, prepared to console her. On the contrary, she was happy.

'How was the class?' I asked her casually.

'It was quite wonderful. I learnt more dishes while teaching. Whatever said and done, it is true that one never stops learning. Every day, everyone enjoyed the food. They never had lunch in their house. All eleven of us used to sit and eat like one big family. After the class, they bought me an *ilkal* sari [a sari deemed special in North Karnataka] as a gift. I don't know why Anand is so upset. I added ten more friends to my friends' circle.'

For this logic of Amba's, I had no answer.

There are people who have published their cookbooks and made money, but our Amba was of a different kind.

It may be possible to have expertise and business sense together, but Amba could never combine the two.

A few days later, Amba became ill with typhoid—a bout that lasted a month. At first, Anand was not bothered about food. He subscribed to a tiffin from an Udupi restaurant. But after three days, he felt it contained too much rice. So, he started getting the tiffin from North Karnataka Restaurant. After the fourth day, he felt the food was loaded with spices, so, he stopped. Then he started buying rotis and sabjis from the Annapoorna store. When masala bun, vada pav, Iyengar Bakery bread . . . none of it had helped him, he realized that the best way was to cook at home—something he had never done before. Normally, no man in North Karnataka ever entered the kitchen. For him, it was like trying to land on the moon. Anand didn't know where the masalas were. With great difficulty, he cooked rice. Even the dog around his house refused to eat it.

The next day, he made chapati. The donkey behind his house did not even sniff at it.

He made sambar. When he looked at it, he lost his appetite.

The more he cooked, the hungrier he became.

After a week, he fell sick. Within fifteen days, nobody knew who was sicker, Amba or Anand. He suffered from loose motion and gas.

Whenever he slept, he dreamt of puranpoli, dosa, idli, paratha, naan, paneer, gobi-paneer and gobi manchurian. But when he opened his eyes, there was nothing.

He understood now that without good food, a man could not survive. All these days, his wife would make different dishes in different seasons and take care of his health. More than Amba, he prayed to God. 'Let my wife recover fast.'

Anand's nature has changed. The other day, I went to their house, as usual with two days' advance notice.

Anand, holding a book in his hand, said, 'Amba, today, the sambar was great. Will you make methi paratha tonight?' I guess he had realized the importance of good cooking along with Kannada literature in his life.

The other day I was travelling by train, and it was raining. I was in my compartment when I suddenly heard my name being called out. I was surprised. It was almost 10 p.m.

It was Amba with a lunch box. She said, 'Nali, I knew that you are going by this train tonight because Anand is also leaving from here. I made a special meal for him and thought of you, and so carried an additional box. I am sure you will enjoy it.'

I looked at her. Though she was tired, she was smiling. She was wet despite holding an umbrella. As she had come running, her heartbeat was high, but her affection was higher.

Thanks and *dhanyavad* don't suffice for the people who are dear to us, who always think of us. A big warm hug or a pat on the back and accepting a person as they are is more than a thanks or a dhanyavad.

I hugged Amba.

11

Made for Each Other

In my town, if there were a competition for the most made-for-each-other couple, Vittal and Vani would have won the first prize with unanimous votes. However, despite their admirable compatibility, they were not well-liked. Theirs was not a love marriage. But the way they thought and the way they complemented each other was so perfect that it made you think that God must have arranged for their match in heaven and made it happen on earth. Sometimes, I wonder, what is God's game? Are we simply puppets in his hands?

They were the opposites of Parvati and Banabhatta in terms of compatibility, but the whole basis of their life was money. They always talked about it and thought about it all the time.

So, I went to their place only rarely. Unfortunately, they were related to us and also to Bindu.

Once, my mother wanted to invite them to the Ganapati festival. I was very reluctant to go to their home to invite them and so I started giving reasons. 'O, I have a lot of homework!' I said.

'Rarely does she do her homework, so let her do that. You go!' my grandmother said to my mother.

'I have a lot of home chores. Why don't you go?' Nali's mother said.

'I am old, and I can't. But I know why both of you are giving excuses not to go to their house.'

Everybody hesitated a little to visit Vittal and Vani's home.

Then my grandmother looked at me, and said, 'Nali, you better go. I will give you an extra laddoo.'

The thought of the extra laddoo made me abandon my homework and visit their home.

The couple was sitting outside the main house under the shade of a tree. They were quite relaxed. Vani bai was wearing a lot of gold ornaments, the kind I had seen only in movies. I had never seen men wearing a lot of gold, but Vittal was also wearing a thick chain and bracelet made of gold. His shirt buttons were gold, too. There were lots of rings on his fingers. I wondered, if he had more fingers, would he have worn more?

They were discussing a wedding. When I went over, they said, 'Nali, sit down.'

Vani asked, 'Nali, did you go to Nandish Patil's wedding?'

Normally, children are innocent and answer whatever questions are asked by anyone. Elders, by experience, are smart enough to answer only when and how they want. So, it was easier for her to extract information from me.

'Of course. The food was excellent,' I replied happily, forgetting about my reluctance in visiting their home.

'I am not asking about the menu. I am just verifying how much gold Suman must have got from her parents.'

Vittal looked at me and said, 'Nali will never understand. In their family, they don't respect gold. Very unusual.'

'Well, I think at least a hundred tolas of gold must have been there.'

'One hundred is too little. Nandish is such a rich party.'

'Nandish does not have a party,' I interrupted.

'Nali, you don't understand. Tell me, why have you come?'

'Come to our home for the Ganapati festival, which is taking place over the next five days.'

'That's fine Nali. You can go now.'

I ran back. They were inhospitable to a child who had come to invite them. But that was their way of living.

The other day, Bindu went to invite them for the release of a Kannada book. He told me about his experience. 'I went to Vani bai's house to share an invitation. My friend Veerabhadra has published a collection of poems with great difficulty, and I promised him an audience. I was completely sure that they won't come, but I always have hope. But the moment they saw the invitation they were quite upset. They said, "Bindu, don't you have a brain? Some fellow writes a poem. Others buy it. Why should you waste money on books? If you read it once, its utility is over. But look at gold. If you buy once, you can use it forever.'''

Vittal came up with a new theory, 'If somebody is so keen to read, they should go to the library and save all the money for extra things and to buy gold.'

'What did you say, Bindu?' I asked.

'I told them no wonder Kannada writers do not make much when rich people like you have this kind of a belief. Their values are so different from the rest of us.'

The couple were relatively rich in our town. They had a car business. They owned a car and some lands, and employed a driver, a cook and a gardener. They preferred to remain confined to their social circle and didn't mix with others. In their list, Hema aunty never found a place.

Vittal and Vani grew up rich. They kept an eye on all their accounts all the time. Such was their privilege that they never understood the helplessness of people. They worried that if they were friendly, someone would ask for money.

Twice a year, on the occasions of *Ugadi* (new year) and *Durgashtami*, they invited people to their home, which otherwise remained closed to visitors. Normally, Vani bai liked to wear a lot of gold but on these two occasions, the way she dressed up was comical. She wore almost 2 kg of gold on her body because she wanted to display her riches. She would give each person a coconut and talked and behaved as if she has done a great thing. Many people skipped this function, but Janaki would never miss it so that she could talk about it for a month.

People still invite the couple to their celebrations because of their proximity and neighbourly courtesy. But Vani and Vittal never go because they feel it is below their dignity.

Once, I saw Janaki near the milk booth. She was standing with Jayant and Bindu. They looked like they were discussing an important matter. I went to buy milk and stood next to them. Though my grandparents didn't like them, I was quite fond of them.

Janaki was saying, 'Yesterday morning, Shyam Rao's mother, who lived opposite Vani bai's house, passed away. It must have been 5 a.m. Immediately, I called Hema, took a rickshaw and went to their house. Poor Shyam Rao was upset and crying. After all, whatever said and done, she was his mother, however old.'

'What about his wife?' asked Jayant.

She reduced her voice by a decibel. 'I thought she was very happy.'

I asked, 'Does that mean your daughters-in-law will be happy when you also die?'

'Shut up, Nali. I didn't realize you were listening to this. Keep quiet. When you become a daughter-in-law, you will understand. Go home now. Take the milk. They will be waiting for it to make tea.'

I didn't go and kept standing. The three continued the conversation. 'Anyway, I thought Prema was beaming with satisfaction. Since nobody else was there, I thought it would be a good idea to walk up to Vittal and Vani bai. After all, they are neighbours and have a social obligation.'

'You did the wrong thing, Janaki. Have you ever called such people who never help?' said Jayant.

'I know from a long time . . .' Bindu started.

'Bindu, don't start with history,' Janaki stopped him.

'What happened Janaki?' Jayant wanted to know more.

'When I rang the bell, I saw a light in their upstairs bedroom.' Janaki knows the layouts of everyone's homes. 'But the minute I called out to them, the light was switched off and they never opened the door. What kind of people are they? When they die, I am sure that not even four people will come for their final rites. There may not be anybody at the funeral at all!'

'Businesspeople are like that,' Jayant said. 'If their neighbours were of their status, they would have opened the door.'

'Don't talk of business. I know what is what . . .'

The conversation went on. Then, I realized that if I didn't go home, I would invite the wrath of my mother, so I ran.

There might have been some exaggeration in that story, but I could believe they would not have opened the door. They never helped anybody. If someone went to their house by mistake, the security guard Govinda always said, 'Let me check if they are inside. They had gone out.' He knew very well of their whereabouts, of course. But if the couple didn't want to meet the person, he would return to say that they are not home. If someone visited their house, they could not go past the verandah. They had to stand or sit depending on their age, the purpose of the visit and their economic background.

Miser Jeevaraj was also very attached to money, but he wouldn't spend it on anyone, including himself. Whereas this couple would spend a tremendous amount on themselves, but not a rupee on anyone else. They had the latest cars and fashionable saris. They bought whatever was available in the market.

Yet their home sorely lacked hospitality. Many times, I thought it was nicer to go to Mulla sabi's or Virupaksha Gowda's homes rather than Vani bai's. Mulla sabi was a poor farmer. His wife Peerambi was very kind and talked to us in Urdu mixed with Kannada. Even though they stayed in a small hut, whenever I visited them, she put mehndi on my hand and gave me a banana and tender coconut. At the house of Virupaksha Gowda, who worked as a clerk in the school, his wife never let me return with an empty stomach. She said, 'Nali, you must eat what I have made for you today.' There would be some savouries, brinjal and sabji. Millet rotis were always kept aside for me. She would say, 'Tell me the story of the latest movie you have seen. Or tell me what you have read.'

Their affection was unparalleled.

Coming back to Vittal and Vani, the couple was blessed with two children—Lakshmi and Shripati. They completed their graduation but were not passionate about anything. Brought up in a fort-like house, talking about money all the time, they never learnt common sense.

Shripati grew up to be a spineless young man. His real test arrived when Vani bai said that she wanted a daughter-in-law. Their conditions were quite strict. They wanted a girl who was not from a poor family as they thought she would take advantage of their wealth and give money to her parents. But they also didn't want a girl from a very rich family because she may not respect them. She had to be very good-looking, extremely obedient to them and from a similar background. She should not have too many brothers and sisters.

Janaki said, 'It is a better idea to pray to God and order him to make a special girl for Shripati. At least in North Karnataka, we don't have anyone like that.'

Neither did they ask in the neighbourhood, nor did anyone want to help them. My grandmother gave strict instructions to Jayant and Bindu, 'Don't get into this.'

But Bindu ignored my grandmother's wisdom and enthusiastically suggested an alliance for Shripati, a girl from Bijapur, which was a far-off land for us.

Shoba was the daughter of Venkob Rao, a big landlord, and their family's status matched Vani bai's. Though their list of wants was endless—1 kg of gold, 5 kg of silver, a great wedding—Venkob Rao agreed to them all.

Bindu was scared. 'Venkya, don't agree to everything. Just check whether you can give in to their demands. These are greedy people. The boy is good, but Vani bai is no ordinary woman. Shoba should not suffer.'

'Don't worry, Bindu. Shoba was brought up in a village that is frequently drought stricken. She knows how to handle all kinds of situations. It will be fine.'

Bindu kept quiet.

The wedding took place according to Vani bai's wishes. She had no complaints. For a change, Vani bai invited Bindu for lunch. It was the first time that he saw her dining room.

'All is well that ends well,' said Jayant.

For the first few months, Shoba agreed to whatever the mother-in-law would say. Vani bai, who never respected Bindu, said openly, 'In life, he did one good thing. He got me a good daughter-in-law.'

One day, Shoba told her in-laws, 'We would like to go to Ooty. I have not seen it. Can we go? On the way, I will go to Bengaluru. My brother has a puja, so I will also meet him.'

Vani bai said, 'Take your ornaments and show your sister-in-law and relatives how well off you are. Take the best of the saris too, but don't leave them in your brother's home.'

Shoba sincerely agreed, 'Whatever you say, mother, I will do accordingly.'

The road from Hubli to Bengaluru was under repair so they decided they would buy a first-class train ticket. The plan was to reach Bengaluru and then hire a cab to Ooty.

Vani bai and her husband said bye to the young couple at the station.

However, the couple returned within two days. Their faces were pale. Shoba started crying. Shripati narrated the reason behind their grief. Another couple was also travelling in first class with them. Shoba kept all her ornaments in a special bag. When they got down to Bengaluru, the suitcase was missing, and the couple had vanished somewhere mid-journey. All the gold had vanished.

The son had been asked to guard the bags. It was not the daughter-in-law's fault. Shoba had told her husband to keep an eye on the bag.

After a few weeks, the grapevine buzzed again. 'It is really not true! Venkya had taken a heavy loan for the extravagant wedding. Shoba was aware of it and had promised to help her father. So, she purposely faked the tragedy and sent all the gold to her parents so that he could repay his loans.'

No one pitied Vani bai. They thought she deserved this.

Now, Shoba started spreading her wings. She was very sharp and was well-trained by her cunning father. She could lie about anything without inhibition. Though Vittal and Vani were fond of money, they were not liars. Thus, they were unable to adjust to Shoba's attitude.

One day, Shobha simply said, 'We want to separate. Anyway, we have property.'

'What property?' said Vittal.

Coolly, she replied, 'I know my husband has a lot of property in his name.'

They had put several properties under Shripati's name to save tax. Taking advantage of this move, Shoba separated from her in-laws.

Bindu was surprised. 'Nali, I have known Shoba for a long time, but I did not know her depths. She is like the Pacific Ocean, so deep.'

Janaki was very happy. 'It is good in one way. Now all her status will dwindle. Money has been divided. Don't you think the circumstances resemble a television soap?'

Jayant said, 'If they have invested in the business properly, they can still make money.' But nobody bothered about his comments, especially when it came to business.

Shoba's house was always open. Anybody could visit her and share food. Lots of her cousins stayed with her. Shoba became arrogant with her new status.

Bindu told us one day that he had been shopping in Hubli Broadway when he encountered Shoba. She pretended to not even recognize him. 'I was the one who fixed their wedding, but she behaved as if she didn't know me,' he cried. 'The shopkeeper asked her to wait, but Shoba demanded immediate attention and service. She was very upset and said, "What do you think? I will wait for you? I can buy this entire shop."'

The shopkeeper was happy because the store was not doing well, and he was searching for a new owner. Shoba provided him with an opportunity.

Thus, Shoba started spending money to satisfy her ego.

In contrast, Vittal and Vani bai felt as if they were drowning.

They were also thinking of their daughter Lakshmi's marriage. The conditions were different—the boy should be good-looking, have a good business, preferably from the city (they didn't want a boy with Shobha's qualities) and his parents should not live with them. Vittal wanted his daughter to have house help, but he did not want her to work.

At last, they found a boy who fit their demands albeit with a few modifications. He had his business but insisted he couldn't stay away from his parents.

Lakshmi's wedding took place. However, she was soon influenced by Shoba's extravagant spending. She joined with her mother-in-law in a coup. She felt even she should get an equal share. When some unknown girl could come and rule the house like a queen, why not her?

Every time she went home, she would ask for something.

'Give me a Mercedes Benz car; my status will be good.'

'Buy me a bungalow in Bengaluru. I will go for a holiday.'

Her demands kept increasing.

Her in-laws were greedy. 'In our family, we do not buy diamonds. Only parents should give. Please give her a diamond set,' they once said.

Slowly, the money started withering away. Neither Shripati nor Lakshmi brought solace to their parents. Now none of their friends bothered to help them.

Vani bai would always look down upon people who worked. She would say, 'Our life is not like others. We don't depend on work. Goddess Lakshmi has injured her feet and she is in our house permanently.'

We realized that a rejuvenated Lakshmi had walked out of the house.

12

Sharada the Fortunate

The name Sharada invoked negative feelings among many people in our town. 'Oh, you met Sharada in the morning? Don't expect much out of your day then. No work can be done,' was a comment you would hear about her often.

Sharada was my distant relative. She was so good-looking. Bindu called her Chittor Padmini of Hubli (Chittor Padmini was the most beautiful queen in history) and I used to call her Vyjayanthimala of Hubli (Vyjayanthimala was one of the most beautiful actresses of yesteryear.) She had long hair that went below her knees and almost touched her feet. When she smiled, dimples formed on her cheeks. She had a good height and perfect features with distinctive, beautiful black eyes. Her image for me was that of innocence. Her father was a peon in the postal department—they were very poor. He was blessed with five daughters, with Sharada being the middle one.

She was fairly good at studies, and so, my grandmother helped her attend college. Seeing her beauty, her father admitted her to a women's college. Still, she received a lot of love letters, which her father had to bring, unfortunately. Her father was trying to marry off his first daughter: however, the prospective grooms would only be interested in Sharda. Bindu would say, 'If there are five bogies in a train, how can you detach the middle one?'

One day, Sharada got an excellent proposal from one Rajesh Desai. His father was a big landlord, and he had a large family. Rajesh and Umesh were the last bachelors of their family. They already had two daughters-in-law and four sons-in-law. Rajesh and Umesh were entrepreneurs—a term used in my town to describe anyone who does not do anything of their own but comes from a business-class family.

When the proposal arrived, everyone was happy because it was a rich family. Her unmarried older sisters were extremely jealous of Sharada's prospects. In a way, they were also relieved because, if Sharada was married off, their path would clear. In those days, looks and money were the only criteria for marriage.

As a custom of arranged marriages of those days, the prospective groom would visit the prospective bride at her home. So, a lot of people from the Desai family came to see Sharada.

As there were not many chairs in Sharada's house, they borrowed a bench from the neighbour. Sharada served the tea but never came to know who the boy was. She never had the courage to ask anybody, but I was already there, omnipresent as ever. Sharada called me and whispered, 'Hey, Nali, who is the boy?'

'Can I go and ask?' I asked overenthusiastically.

'Don't be silly. Just find out.'

The ten-year-old me was playing an important role in twenty-year-old Sharada's life. I went quietly and asked loudly, 'Who is the boy, ajji?'

Everybody laughed. Mrs Desai pointed to the corner of a bench, where the two boys were sitting. I went and told Sharada, 'Shari, I think one of those two boys.' Shari peeped out of the window. She was very happy. One of the boys was extremely handsome. Anyway, her opinion did not matter much in the marriage. It was a decision that would be heavily based on financial constraints. Sharada's father did not need to spend any money.

The wedding took place in the Desais' large house, the Desai Wada. There were a handful of people from Sharada's side; the rest were all from the Desai clan. When Sharada went to garland her husband, she saw him for the first time. Her face paled and she started trembling. Her husband was not the one she had identified as her groom, but a crude-looking man. Rajesh was chosen to be her husband. She saw the handsome Umesh and realized he was his younger brother. Though she liked him, now he had to be her Lakshman.

Everybody congratulated Sharada and her father. The Desais served a very heavy lunch but there were a lot of comments. Ganga said, 'There must be something wrong with the boy, otherwise why would a Desai marry a poor girl like Sharada?' In her heart, she knew that Sharada was better-looking than her.

Janaki thought she was whispering in Bindu's ear, but everybody could hear, 'I hear that he doesn't have a job and depends on his father's income. There is no real business. I also heard that the boy does not have a good character. They got this girl to stop his "extra" activities.'

Bindu added his two bits. 'These things do happen. A capable queen can rule a kingdom when the husband is weak. Who knows, Sharada may become the queen of this wada.' Wada, in local parlance, is commonly used for a big house (sometimes of an ancestral quality) with many floors and a main gate. The Desais' house was like a mini palace with a big compound.

My grandmother got very angry and said, 'All three of you keep quiet. We have come to a wedding, let us bless her to lead a happy life.'

Months passed. We never saw Sharada step out of the wada. However, we would see Rajesh on and off. I would always ask him, 'How is Shari? I've not seen her at all since marriage. Can I come and see her?'

Rajesh would give vague answers. 'She is fine. Come sometime. I'm very busy now. I am on a business tour. I'm going to Mumbai and Pune.' This was his standard answer. We came to know that Sharada never visited her parents' house. We did not know whether she didn't want to go or they never allowed her to go. My grandmother used to get upset. 'What is Rajesh doing all the time, business? I think she is a captive in their house.'

'Shall I go and meet her?' I asked.

'They are very reserved people. What reason will you give to go to their house?' my mother asked.

My grandmother said, 'Nali is a young girl. We can say someone had gone to Tirupathi and had sent a ladoo. Let Nali take it and go to their house. Nobody can stop her.' And so, Tirupathi Balaji became the reason for me to enter the fortress of this wada.

The wada was filled with people. On one side, men sat leisurely eating paan and smoking. On the other side, women were busy oiling and combing their hair and cleaning their ornaments. I did not see Sharada anywhere. The senior Desai's wife almost scolded me, 'Why have you come?'

For a minute, I was scared. Then I took courage and said, 'I'm the granddaughter of Krishnakka. Ajji has sent Tirupathi prasad for Sharada.'

The moment Mrs Desai heard Krishna and prasad, she said, 'Go to the kitchen and distribute the prasad.' When I went, I was surprised to see Sharada. She was in an ordinary saree, sitting and grating the coconut. She looked frail, colourless and had an extremely unhappy expression on her face. The gold bangles, which were given to her during her wedding, now went back to her elbow. She was happy to see me. She embraced me and tears started flowing. 'How is everyone in my house and your house? I have not met anyone for the last six months.' She wiped her tears and said, 'Nali, will you tell your ajji to send me an invite for dinner sometime? I want to come to your house and cry.'

'Why cry?' I asked innocently.

'You don't understand but your grandmother will. Now run away otherwise my mother-in-law will come to know what I'm talking to you about,' she told me in a hushed voice. She was right. I could see Mrs Desai coming towards the kitchen.

'What is there to say to this little girl, Sharada? There are so many guests today, better help in the kitchen.' She looked at me and said, 'You can go now.'

I ran back home. I went and repeated Sharda's message to my grandmother, without bothering that I was getting late for school. Ajji was surprised. She told my mother, 'I knew something is wrong; that's the reason the girl is not coming out of her home. Her father is not bothered. He has to marry off another girl. At times I feel, her beauty was a curse to her.'

'Is beauty a curse, ajji?' I interrupted.

'Don't interfere in elders' talk; go to school.' My mother pushed me out. In our house, women were the decision-makers. Men were the supportive acts.

The next day my mother went to Desai Wada and said, 'We have a family feast on the coming Sharad Poornima. So, please send your son and daughter-in-law for the moonlight dinner.'

My mother returned and described what had happened. Mrs Desai had invited her in with respect because my father was a doctor. A doctor's wife is respected in a village. Mrs Desai then went on to describe their wealth and stated that Sharada was lucky. She told my mother that since Sharada was not used to a rich life, it would take time for her to adjust and she doesn't have any objection to her coming to our house and staying overnight if the dinner is late, provided Rajesh agrees.

'I know that Rajesh will not come,' ajji said. 'I don't know whether they'll send Sharada. Poor girl. She has to tell someone what she's feeling, only then she'll be destressed. We cannot give gold and silver to ease someone's problems, but we can lend our ears to somebody's difficulties.'

My grandfather was normally a man of few words. But now he spoke. 'In case Sharada talks about her difficulties to you, see that it does not reach her mother-in-law. She will make Sharda's life difficult. I have a request to you, don't call Janaki, Ganga, Bindu . . . your gang. Let us limit it to family only.'

That evening Sharada came home. My mother and grandmother took her to a small room upstairs. Sharada was crying uncontrollably. I was not allowed inside but my curious nature compelled me to spy through the slit of the window. Sharada said, 'Name the bad habits; my husband has them all. He just does not care for me. My father was sold with their money. I was a burden to everybody at home. My beauty was a problem for my other sisters. Now, I'm not respected in my in-law's house because my husband doesn't care for me. He finds fault in whatever I do. He has no patience with me.'

'Sharada, you know why he doesn't care?' ajji said. 'Because he doesn't love you. Why does he discover a mistake and doesn't have patience with you? Because he doesn't have affection for you. Where there is love and affection there will be patience. Any mistake you make, the person will accept it. Patience is connected to affection. The faults are thick when love is thin.'

Days passed.

Sharada was widowed after Rajesh died of a disease. His death seemed imminent as it arrived despite the family spending quite a bit on doctors and treatments. Sharada was eventually blamed for the fatality. Her in-laws kept saying that she had brought bad luck, that they had probably been given a wrong horoscope. Her parents didn't want her back home and so, her in-laws turned her into a worker. She became like a coolie without a salary. She had to help look after children, iron the heavy silk sarees of her sisters-in-law, help them with their grooming etc. The only fellow who felt bad for her was the youngest brother, Umesh. He was an engineer. Sometimes he would tell his mother, 'Why trouble her, she's already lost her husband. Give her some space and time to recover.'

His mother got upset with Umesh and said, 'You don't know anything about women, so don't talk. You know, in mythology, Savitri who lost her husband reached out to the God of death and got his life back. If Sharada would have served her husband and prayed to God sincerely, we would not have lost our son. We are large-hearted people, so we are keeping her in our house.'

Then, the Desai family decided to go on a Badrinath and Kedarnath yatra. The entire family left, with Sharada accompanying them for all the domestic help. But alas, they could not complete the pilgrimage. They returned to our town after a great tragedy.

When the group was in Rishikesh buying gifts, the senior Desai realized that he didn't have enough money for the purchase. They were on the other side of the famous Lakshman Jhula, a special bridge made up of iron wire. It is very well-known that whosoever goes to Rishikesh has to cross it. The senior Desai called his daughter-in-law Sharada, 'Take this key and go to the other side. Your mother-in-law is sleeping in the other room. Give her the keys; she'll give you money. Bring it back.' Though they used to scold Sharada for everything, they knew she was an honest person. He would not have sent his other daughters-in-law for this work. Sharada took the keys and had just left when The senior Desai realized that sending her alone might not be a good idea.

He called out to Umesh, 'Go with her. There might be some thieves along the route. It's better for a man to accompany her.' While they were walking on the Lakshman Jhula, a powerful storm hit the Ganga flowing underneath and the bridge turned upside down. For a couple of minutes, there was a lot of dust in everybody's eyes, which sparked commotion on both sides of the bridge. Once the scene cleared out, the spectators saw the bridge swinging without people.

Everybody was happy that the storm had subsided. The senior Desai assumed that Umesh and Sharada had crossed the bridge. He returned to his wife and told her that Sharada and Umesh were coming for the keys. 'I hope Umesh was ahead of Sharada and had crossed the bridge. What happened to Sharada? Did she fall?' There was a kind of anxiety was in his voice.

Mrs Desai was more horrified. 'No, it is not like that. Sharada was ahead and my child Umesh was behind her. She might have escaped this storm. Oh! my child, Umesh!' She started crying loudly at the conjecture.

However, people around them said they were in the middle of the bridge and did not make it to the end. The senior Desai was suddenly shrouded with surety—his anxiety turned into grief. He collapsed on to the ground. His handsome, young son along with his widowed daughter-in-law had fallen from the Lakshman Jhula. He saw the mighty Ganga flowing below. With teary eyes, he searched for two heads in the water and prayed to the river to spare his son at least.

River Ganga originates from Vishnu's feet and goes from there to Shiva's head and later to Jahnu's ear. Nobody can control her. She is eternal. The Desais sent some people to search for both bodies but could not find them. People consoled them. Then, the Desais came back empty-handed and performed the shraddha.

Years passed, and nobody bothered about Sharada. Only my grandmother shed tears. With a sigh, she said, 'Anyway, she got mukti.'

Time strode on.

Like any other Hubli girl, I got married and had children. They went abroad for their work, and I lost my grandparents and parents. The Desai family was broken into pieces. They lost their land in tenancy and the wada was sold for money. The family left the village and became clerks in the city. Now, there's a big Lulu Mall in the wada's place and no one remembers the past.

As I grew old, I decided to do a pilgrimage to Badrinath and Kedarnath. However, I was scared to go to Rishikesh because it always reminded me of Sharada. But an adventurous group of friends decided to go and so I went.

We reached Rishikesh. I visited the Lakshman Jhula with tears in my eyes, lost in memories of Sharada, my grandmother and my mother. On our way to Badrinath, one of my friend's brothers, who was posted in Auliya, invited us to his home for a couple of days. In the evening, he took us to the Auliya Club. There were many people, and we were having a great time when someone came up to me, and said to me in Kannada, 'Nali, how are you?' I looked up at a lady who appeared familiar, but I wasn't able to place her. She laughed and two dimples formed on her cheeks. I looked at her hair. It wasn't as long, but still long, with a hint of salt and pepper in it.

I said, 'Shari!'

'Of course, Ganga Rao,' she told me.

That night I told my friends I would spend the night with Shari and join them the next day. On the balcony of her house, Sharada and I sat for a few minutes without talking, with tears in our eyes.

Sharada started telling her story. 'When the storm hit Lakshman Jhula on that auspicious day, the air entered my petticoat and it turned into a parachute. To save me, Umesh was holding my hand and both of us flew with the hurricane. It took us a long distance and threw us in a field. Both of us were saved. Then, I told Umesh that I didn't want to go back. I asked him to leave me there. I said I would have to live like a coolie and spend my life on the Ganga's banks. "You can go back and say I was dead. This is the only favour I want from you."

'Umesh was quiet for some time and said, "Both of us could have died in the Ganga. When fate has saved us together, let us live together. I never dared to fight the system and my parents back in town. I don't want to leave you here. You are the bride that destiny has given me."

'There was a Vishnu temple in the village, and we were married there. He renamed me Ganga and changed his name to D. Umesh Rao.'

Sharada's story was so unbelievable that even in a movie they would not think of such an ending. Sharada continued, 'We have only one son and we have named him Lakshman. He works in Delhi. As Umesh was an engineer, he got a job in the Gadwal district after our marriage. He has retired now. My daughter-in-law is also from Gadwal and now we are more Gadwalis. We have built a house here. I thank God immensely. We talk Kannada at home, but outside there is nobody.'

'But why did you not come back to our town at least once?'

'How could we come back? People would have been upset with our marriage and ostracised us. And the Desais are powerful people.'

I laughed and told her the story of the Desais and their gradual downfall.

She shed tears.

The next morning the car came for me to join my friends.

Sharada came down to see me off. She handed me a small box. It was a pair of earrings.

I said, 'Shari, I don't want this. I met you and that is enough. Come to Bangalore. The world has changed now.'

'Nali, do you remember that one Sharad Poornima your ajji had called me for dinner? She wasn't a psychologist, but she knew that I was in pain and needed to talk and pour it out. She also gave me the definition of patience and told me that patience is proportionate to love and affection. Nali, it is a great message. My husband loves me even today as much as he did when we got married. Our affection is deep for each other.'

I remembered that at the bride-viewing function, I had pointed out Umesh as the boy who had come to see Shari. She had been so happy. Maybe it was providence that I introduced them the first time. Ajji, I thought, wherever you are, please bless Shari. In reply to that, there was a mild shower. I presume it was my ajji's tears of joy.

13

Chami the Charmer

Chami was short, squint-eyed and a little plump. She was not academically bright but very shrewd. I never saw Chami aunty talk negatively about anybody. She always spoke nicely even about people like Ganga, who brimmed with pride.

'Don't believe Chami,' said Janaki. 'She is not even like a bitter gourd. It is at least good outside and bad inside. This one is bad both inside and out.'

Bindu said that she would have been a diplomat if she were in a king's court.

Amba said, 'She sits in the verandah like a chowkidar all the time. Does she ever cook?'

Hema aunty said, 'Why should we bother? Let her live the way she wants.'

Bindu knew Chami's history.

Chami was born into a family of moneylenders. Her mother was simple, but her father Veerabhadra was a very strong personality and an adamant man. She learnt lots of life skills from him but had the advantage of a sweet tongue, which he did not have. Her mother was the namesake head of the family, but it was young Chami who ruled the home. When she came to be of marriageable age, Veerbhadra set out to look for a groom. He was ready to spend lots of money on her marriage, but no one asked for her hand.

Veerabhadra had a distant cousin named Anant who had two sons. Veerbhadra approached him with a marriage alliance for Chami. Both these men were in the same profession and had known each other for a long time. They were good friends. But both Anant's sons rejected the proposal and Anant had to apologise.

Anant had lots of money. He had a younger brother who would help him in his work. But he had died in an accident. The younger brother's wife, Sumathi, did not have any children. Anant requested her to stay on. 'Sumathi, you have brought up my children and you are like a mother to them. Don't go.' But she disagreed. Her brother was an advocate in Pune, and she went to live with him. Anant would send some money for her maintenance.

The advocate brother took this opportunity to influence his sister on what she was due from her marital home. 'Sumathi, whatever said and done, they are not your children. Your husband also worked hard with Anant. You should get half the share in the property.'

Sumathi did not agree initially. She was alone and thought it did not matter. But the lure of money changed her mind. She sent a letter to Anant for a half share in the property. Anant broke into a tandava nritya after receiving it. It was extremely hard for him to part with his property. He sat down with an advocate, who was also a friend and made other plans. 'Most of my assets are in the form of gold. I have kept all that in this iron safe.'

The advocate advised, 'Shift the locker somewhere in the night. Let us create some backdated false document stating that you have a big loan. Let the Pune advocate come, and we can show those loan documents.'

But where could he shift the locker so quickly? It was not an easy job. Then Anant thought of Veerbhadra.

He went to his house and requested he keep the locker for a few months. 'I will also give you money. Will you keep it in your house?'

Veerabhadra thought for a few minutes and agreed. That night, with great difficulty, they shifted the locker from Anant's house to Veerbhadra's.

After a week, Sumathi and her advocate arrived from Pune. Sumathi was surprised to see the house without the locker. Moreover, Anant proved that they never had any safe. He also produced a lot of loan papers, saying, 'If you take half the property, then you have to take half the loan as well.' The Pune lawyers were defeated. They returned to Pune with Sumathi. Anant was relieved and stopped sending her monthly expenses.

The very next day, Anant went to Veerabhadra's house and thanked him for his help. He asked, 'Can I take my locker back?'

'You can take it back,' Veerabhadra said patiently, 'the keys are with you. I have not opened the locker. But along with your locker, you have to take my daughter also. It is the fees. You can take her as your daughter-in-law for any one of your sons. It is your choice.'

The proposition shocked Anant. If they didn't comply, they would lose their entire property. Though furious, he was a serpent without fangs. Finally, he called his sons, and said, 'Whoever marries her will get 70 per cent of the money. The other one will get 30 per cent.'

The second son opted for 30 per cent and thus, Chami came to Anant's house with the locker.

No one liked Chami, including her husband, Nagendra. Chami never took part in anything and would remain invested in herself. She would go to the temple every day, sit on the bench in their verandah and observe people. Once in a while, she would talk to children and extract information from them. She was a storehouse of news but never broadcast it. She was a machine where there was only input and no output, unlike Janaki who was a broadcaster, with less input and more output.

Chami's strength was strategizing her way through life. Bindu would say that Chami had fabricated her wedding strategy and told her father to execute it.

Janaki said Chami was a charmer. Her speech was as sweet as nectar, but her mind was as sharp as a knife.

Nagendra danced to her tunes all the time. 'If there was ever a movie called *Joru ka Ghulam*, Chami is the joru and Nagendra the ghulam,' said Ganga.

The other day when I was returning from school, Chami called me. 'Come Nali, sit down. Your hair is so beautiful. You should wear jasmine every day. You look like Saraswati.' I was on cloud nine, knowing well that my hair was short. 'Maybe I will tell your teacher to make you Bharat Mata on Independence Day. She is my cousin. Do you want to eat ladoo? Oh, it is noon, so water is better.' She patted me on my back and I felt relaxed.

Though my mother and grandmother love me a lot, they never sat next to me; they didn't say I looked like Saraswati or Bharat Mata. On the contrary, they delivered sermons regularly—study well, do puja and the Goddess will be kind to you. Chami was the only person who talked about my beauty. I was incredibly happy.

Chami's questions started now, 'Nali, the other day, so many people came to your house. Was there anything special?'

'Yes, Chami aunty, we had Satyanarayana puja.'

'Who all came?'

'The same gang,' I replied, Janaki, Ganga, Bindu, Hema aunty, Amba, Jayant.'

'But I did not see Jeevraj?'

I was wondering, how with the squint in her eye, she had noticed that Jeevraj hadn't come.

'And your uncle also hadn't come?'

'They went out of station.'

'Where did they go? Together or separately?'

Actually, even I did not know where they had gone.

Chami came out and put a barfi in my hand, 'Eat this, you may remember now.'

'Jeevaraj, maybe to Belgaum, I am not sure.'

'Oh, it might be for a marriage proposal.'

'Oh yes.' After eating barfi I felt more energetic. 'Janaki's son received a marriage proposal from Bengaluru and so my uncle has gone there.'

'Oh, the girl is from Bengaluru. They are soft-spoken, wear silk sarees, and never forget to wear flowers in their hair. I am sure Janaki will understand that. Her children are nice. But still, it will be a different culture.

'The other day, I saw an auto in front of your house. Who had come to your house?"

'Some patient could have come,' I said casually.

Chami wanted to gather information about everyone, from the comfort of her home, through children.

'Does your father practice at home or the hospital?'

'I do not know,' I said.

'But as his child, you may know.'

'I have to go now. I have to play with my dolls.'

'Where did you get your dolls from? Were they gifted or purchased?'

'My father's patients gifted them to me.'

'What other gifts do you get?'

'Sometimes ribbons, sometimes flowers or gifts from my grandmother during Sharad Poornima.'

'No wonder your grandmother performs Sharad Poornima festival and invites so many people. It is a very good custom.'

She wanted to know the guest list, but I wanted to run as the barfi was over.

When I reached home, there was another set of interviews.

Bindu was sitting in front of the house and talking to some women and, as usual, my grandfather was in the study room.

'Nali, why did you come late?'

'On the way back from school, Chami aunty called me in,' I told him.

Bindu was curious now. 'Why did she call you? She must have asked a lot of questions.'

'Yes, she did. How do you know?' I wondered.

'I know everyone's DNA,' Bindu boasted.

'What did she ask?' My mother asked, furious that I had lingered around Chami aunty.

I recounted the whole conversation.

'Why did you have to tell her everything?'

Grandmother tried to intervene. 'After all, she is a kid, kids don't lie,' she said. 'Let her tell.'

I went inside to freshen up and eat something. Though I was having my snack, my ears were outside.

'You know Chami's history?' Bindu asked my mother.

'Oh, regarding that locker, we all know,' my mother said.

'No, not that. Another thing,' Bindu said.

Just then the bell rang, and Ganga and Janaki came in.

Bindu's love of storytelling increased with a larger audience.

All of them settled down comfortably. I went and placed a jug of water with some glasses, and quietly sat in a corner where no one would notice me.

'You know when Chami was married, everyone was upset. But Chami had a honeyed tongue. So, people accepted her in time. When she became pregnant, she told her father-in-law, "I want to go to my father's house for delivery. But my brother's wife is delivering at the same time, so can I call my mother to come here and help me for the next three months? It will be a great favour to me. You are like my father. I will never forget your help."'

Initially, Anant was aloof but later he agreed. Thus, Chami's mother was called.

Chami's mother got along very well with everyone and soon, she became a part of the household. Soon, a baby boy was born.

Anant was very clever. Though there were many gold ornaments in the house, he would let Chami wear them only three or four times a year. When the occasion was over, he would take it back and put it in the locker. He would never leave anything with her.

'Now, you are a grandfather. He is your first grandchild. Don't you think it would be appropriate that I should wear gold for the occasion? Many people will come to the function. If I am devoid of jewellery, it will bring a bad name to you. People will say, "He is such a wealthy man, but look at his daughter-in-law". However, your decision is final,' said Chami.

The honey-talk worked. He felt she was right in saying that people will criticise him. So that day, he gave her half a kilogram of ornaments to wear and told her to return immediately after the function.

It was a big event. Many people said, 'Chami, God is very kind to you. Your in-laws are also rich, and you are fortunate to have so many ornaments. And you have delivered a baby.'

'That is all because my in-laws love me,' said Chami.

When it was time for her to return her ornaments, Chami told her father-in-law, 'Today is Friday. If you want, I can remove everything and give it to you. But elders say this is the time Goddess Lakshmi comes home and we should not remove our ornaments. It will not be good for the elders, family and business. However, I will listen to you.'

Anant pitied Chami as she proceeded to remove the bangles from her hands. Up to this day she had been very obedient. Her marriage had started with enmity and no love. Fortunately, now, her husband had adjusted to her. She had never been harsh to anyone and given the family an heir. Now, she was making a request in the interest of the family. In this weak moment, he agreed and said, 'You can give the jewellery back tomorrow.'

Chami had a separate room known as the delivery room. It was next to the drawing room. The next day, when

Anant was having a bath, he heard a lot of commotion. He rushed out half-bathed, only to find that Channi had been tied to a piece of furniture with a cloth stuffed in her mouth. Their baby was crying. The door of the room was open, and the jewellery box lay open on the floor, emptied of its contents. Chami's mother was sobbing, shouting, 'Thief, thief . . .'

But there was nobody at the front door.

Chami's mother said, 'I was in the kitchen. I came to give milk. A thief came, tied Chami, stuffed her mouth and took away the ornaments. Lots of people assembled after the commotion. All of this took place between 7 a.m. and 8 a.m. It is harrowing that this robbery took place in broad daylight.'

We have heard of such crimes taking place in Pune and Mumbai, but never in Karnataka, because our neighbours are always alert. Some people said that they did notice and some said they were inside, but nobody had said what had exactly happened. Chami's hands were untied, and the cloth was removed from her mouth. 'I wish I had given the gold yesterday itself. It is my fault.'

She touched Anant's feet. He did not say a word.

But Janaki understood and whispered in Bindu's ears, 'This is drama, the second time around.'

Anant also knew it, but there was no proof. Jayant, adding fuel to the fire, asked if he should give a police complaint.

Anant declined.

Chami showed more interest now. 'No, we should do it. Ours is a small town and it is easy to trace them. Let them be punished.'

The crowd melted away. While returning, Janaki asked, 'Do you know why Anant said no and Chami said yes?'

'Why?' I asked.

'Anant is not a simple person. He has ancient gold coins. And if you give a police complaint everything has to be checked. In that case, these coins could go to the museum. Lots of other secrets will also come out. Anant will be checked for black money. It is easier to lose half a kilo of gold, rather than the police finding out about all his possessions. Chami also knew that her father-in-law would not allow it. Thus, she has pressed for the complaint.'

The next day, Chami's mother gave good gifts to the daughter and son-in-law and left.

A few months later, Bindu brought the news that Veerbhadra had purchased a new farm with cash on hand. People wondered how a small moneylender got so rich.

'Chami is goddess Lakshmi to her father,' Janaki said in a hushed tone.

Many years passed after this incident.

The old Chami aunty was sitting on the verandah. On seeing me she called out, 'Nali, come here!'

'How are you?'

'I am fine.'

'Do you want to drink water or eat peda?'

'I will have peda.'

Even though I was grown up now, I will not miss a chance to eat peda at Chami aunty's house. I ate the peda and casually asked Chami aunty, 'You have undergone so many ups and downs in life. How did you manage?'

Chami laughed out loud, and it was the first time ever that I had seen Chami aunty laughing.

'My child, I am not a graduate and I never went to school like you people did. But I have learnt lessons from life. They have given me courage. For instance, you should never speak with the intention to hurt anyone. Your harsh words will be etched in their minds forever, more than your deeds. There is a saying, "*vachana daridrata*", which means don't be stingy with good words. When difficulties grow, you should grow bigger than those difficulties, like Lord Hanuman. You should make a strategy for everything in life and follow it.'

I ate the peda and said, 'Chami aunty, you are a management guru.'

14

Lunch Box Nalini

I am Nalini Kulkarni. Elders have always called me Nali—a typical shortening of the name in North Karnataka. Here, Anand becomes Andya and Mandakini becomes Mandi. No wonder, the transition from Nalini to Nali was effortless.

Until now, I have peeped into everyone's life and written about their characters. Now, let me talk about myself—the best way to joke is not at someone else's expense but at your own.

But how did lunch box get affixed to my name, you may wonder.

As I go about observing everyone's habits and characteristics, I don't get time to cook. That doesn't mean I don't like to eat. I am very fond of eating. If someone calls me for lunch, I not only attend it but also carry my lunch box to carry some food back for my dinner. Whenever I go to any function, all my relatives, without greeting me, say, 'Nalini, fill up your lunch box first. Then you will be at peace, and we can talk at leisure.' That's why I am known as Lunch Box Nalini.

A few days ago, my cousin, Venkat, had his child's naming ceremony. Venkat's wife Veena formally invited me, saying, 'We will be very happy if you come for the naming ceremony. If you don't have time for lunch, at least visit us for half an hour.'

I laughed and said, 'Don't you remember what they call me? I always come for the meal more than the event. I'll be honest with you. If you tell me to come for the event without lunch, then I'm sure that only three people will be there for the naming ceremony—you, your husband and your little bundle of joy.'

Everyone laughed at my comment. Bundle Bindu, who was around, commented about hospitality in different regions.

'I know. Some people's hospitality is the bare minimum unlike in North Karnataka. Because historically . . .'

'Stop it,' I told Bindu.

He ignored me and continued.

'Recently, I had been to someone's house,' Jayant said. 'Wait a minute. I will have tea and come. I will also come and join you for tea.'

'Jaya, you are shameless,' I said.

But by and large, when you invite people, you should do it wholeheartedly. The person should feel welcomed.

I turned to Venkat and said, 'I will come for the function in the morning as I have recently joined as a college lecturer.

I will leave my lunch box there and pick it up on the way back after my classes. I won't be able to make it for lunch, but I can eat it at home, at least.'

'There can be no one like you,' said Jayant.

I take my lunch box along with me to a function if I know the family hosting the event very well. I have several lunch boxes—unbreakable, Tupperware, hot cases and transparent ones. Because they are useful for various dishes—and depending on the circumstance, I change the boxes. For gravies, Tupperware is better. For roti and poli, a hot case is better. For pickles, unbreakable is better and transparent because it is easier to identify what is inside.

I am very fond of lunch boxes. In fact, I am an expert. My refrigerator is filled with different kinds of boxes that came with food from different homes. I can match the boxes and the places that they came in from. Mulla's wife Peerambi's box is yellow, though it is green inside. Virupaksha Gowda's wife Basavaa's *dabba* is made of German steel. It is round and is currently sitting in my fridge with some brinjal. Bhagirati's green plastic box has yellow laddoos inside. Jayant's transparent box has gol gappas.

The other day, when I was eating dinner, I told my daughter, 'There is a gulab jamun from Janaki's home. Though her tongue is bitter, her gulab jamuns are excellent.'

My daughter was confused. 'How do I know which is her box of gulab jamun? There are so many lunch boxes in the refrigerator.'

'Oh, bring the one with a dome-like structure,' I responded easily. 'I didn't have a box with me that day, so she had given me hers.'

While having the gulab jamun, I remembered the dry vegetable. 'Will you open the fridge and get the plastic box with a flat red cover? That is from Ganga's home. A family had visited her with a marriage proposal, so she had specially made a vegetable for the boy, which she also sent me.'

The other day, Bundle Bindu came with a huge box. His wife, Saraswati, was out of station. I opened it and to my surprise, there was a steamed sweet dish inside. It is complicated to make, though my grandmother was particularly good at it. I asked, 'Bindu when Saraswati is not there, how could you cook this special dish?'

Bindu laughed and said, 'Who said that I have made this? There is a famous saying, "When two people are fighting, it is the third one that enjoys."'

'What do you mean?'

Bindu said, 'Suman has sent rice kheer and her mother-in-law has sent bottle gourd kheer. They felt that you are the best judge to decide *who is the better cook* because you are known for tasting dishes. They called me separately and gave me these two boxes. So, you eat and enjoy when both want you to judge their dishes and take their side.'

'Bindu, in that case, I will taste neither of them', I said immediately.

'Nali, please be diplomatic. You can say both are very good, but separately. Then you will have an advantage,' said Jayant, who always thinks of profit and loss.

'No, Jayant. I don't want to do that. Profit and loss are acceptable in business, not in human interaction. All these people are dear to me. Whenever they make something special, they send some to my home even if I don't visit them. I carry my lunch box only to places where I have liberty and affection. If I really want to eat, there are many restaurants in this town. A lunch box is not a mere lunch box. It is a bridge between two people. I go to their home, or they send me some food in it. Then, I go to return the box. Thus, we share feelings and give company to each other. In case any of us are in difficulty, we reduce our tensions. The lunch boxes are nothing but a sign of affection, and it is through them that I have been able to meet people and form a close bond with them over the years. It has been my educational journey into the nature of humanity.

'I don't want to get into the competition between a daughter-in-law and mother-in-law or create more distance between them. If somebody wants to start a fight, I don't want to be a party to that.'

Bindu laughed and said, 'And I know how you love food too!'

I smiled.

'O Nali, you are a typical North Karnataka girl,' said Bindu.

'What do you mean by that?' I was surprised by his comment.

'Straightforward, transparent, loving, sharing, impractical, talkative—that is the essence that the land blesses us with.'

My memories took me back . . .

The other day, I was in a hurry and gave Sheela's dabba to Janaki—her eternal enemy. The next afternoon, in the searing hot sun in May, when no one goes out in the afternoon, Janaki came to my house with open hair and a red face. She reminded me of Draupadi in the Rajya Sabha of Duryodhana at Hastinapura. Immediately, she said, 'Nali, what is inside your head?'

'Please sit down. Let me give you some buttermilk,' I said.

The buttermilk had come from Amba's home. It had ginger, cilantro and other spices that made for a nice, tasty buttermilk. Janaki cooled down after drinking it. She now reminded me of Narasimha after killing Hiranyakashipu. She then repeated her question. 'What is inside your head?'

'As of right now, I don't know. But you can open and see,' I joked.

'This is not a joke. How dare you give that Sheela's box to me? Even more, why are you friendly with her?' she questioned me.

'Janaki, I can't fight with people. Sheela is kind to me. She sent me a good okra vegetable the other day,' I said weakly. 'What is wrong in that?'

'Nali, you don't understand. Don't underestimate her. Sheela must have sent you the leftovers from the previous day. She is not a good lady. How can you accept what she sends to you?'

'It is not true. When the box came, it was fresh and warm,' I answered.

'Nali, you are brainless. She must have heated it in the microwave and sent it to you.'

I brought her another glass of buttermilk. I knew the real reason she was upset. Sheela's daughter did not marry Janaki's son. That had created room for rage. She blamed Sheela every opportunity she got. Unfortunately, today, a box that has stayed with me had brought it up.

Apart from bringing drama into my life, boxes have brought some respite during dull moments.

On a no-moon day, when there are no occasions to attend, I was wondering where to go. That's when Amba came to my house with a lunch box as if answering my prayers. She said, 'I have brought food for two days.'

'Amba, it is raining. Why did you have to come all the way just to give me some food?'

'Nali, I know that you are always reading or writing something. While cooking, I realized that you had nowhere to go since it was a no-moon day. So, I just cooked a little extra.'

'People say North Karnataka has great hospitality. They must have seen you, and not me,' I said. 'Because I have such friends, I can afford to not cook and still stay here. Otherwise, I would have gone to another country by this time.'

A long time ago, when I joined as a temporary lecturer in a college, I had asked for leave to attend my friend Vimla's wedding. However, the principal had refused. So, I told Vimla that I could only come for half an hour.

That day, I went to the wedding ceremony early in the morning and left my new lunch box (which I had purchased from my first salary) in the venue's kitchen. By then, I knew all the good cooks in our area, and they also knew me. The moment I entered the kitchen, the cook smiled and said, 'O Nalini, good you got your lunch box. I will fill it up. Come and take it after 2 p.m., after the reception.'

'What are you going to put in my box?'

He laughed at me and looked at my new lunch box, 'What do you want?'

'I don't want rice and sambar. Put all the other sweets and savouries,' I said and vanished.

Just as I was about to leave at 2 p.m., the principal called me and lectured me on how to be a good teacher. But my mind was at the wedding hall. She finally let me go at 3 p.m. By the time I arrived, there were very few people remaining. All the other important people had gone. The cook told me to collect my lunch box from the corner.

I picked it up and came home.

When I opened it, I got the shock of my life. It was an aluminium lunch box, instead of my new shiny steel lunch box, with lots of dents, indicating its number of years in service. It must have ridden a cycle many times. Apart from that, when I opened it, inside was rice, sambar and rasam. I was about to cry. First of all, I had lost my precious lunch box. Second, I got a bad lunch box in return. Third, the lunch was so ordinary.

I lost my appetite.

I went back to the wedding hall. There was pin-drop silence. I felt that my destiny with my lunch box was like

Kunti's children—whatever they did, they never got the kingdom. Whatever I did, I couldn't find my new lunch box.

The box had four compartments. At the top, I had a small carrier to put butter or ghee. I even got NK, for Nalini Kulkarni, engraved on it. Now this one had only three sections. It had NK written on the top, but it wasn't my name.

I had been sorely defeated.

Little did I know what lay in store for me.

In my time, searching for a groom was a big process. When I was studying, everybody would say, 'Nali is still young. What is the hurry for a groom? Let's see after a few years.'

The day I got my first job, I suddenly felt I had become a liability. Everyone began asking, 'When is Nalini getting married? Are you not searching for boys yet? Hurry up before it's too late for her.'

Janaki made several visits to my home and gave sermons on the supposed evil effects of late marriage to my mother and grandmother. I was baffled.

Many grooms came and I met them in a traditional way but there was a problem every time. One boy said in front of me, 'I want someone like Mala Sinha [a film actress of yesteryears].'

He himself looked like a villain. I secretly wished I could gift him a mirror so he could see his face.

One boy told me, 'I want to get married since my mother wants an assistant to do most of the work.'

So, he wanted me to be an unpaid domestic help.

One boy asked me to sing, '*Mang ke saath tumhara, maang liya sansaar.*'

I refused and instead sang '*Do hanson ka joda bichhad gayo re.*'

As I was the only unmarried girl in a large family, some of my uncles rejected the boys before I could meet them. Many boys failed to reach my family's expectations, mostly because they had overpowering mothers. They were rejected by the women of the family. It seemed we were all like frogs, not staying together and jumping one at a time.

Like any girl, I had my dreams. I didn't like this formal boy-meeting or girl-meeting business. In my dreams, a good-looking prince would arrive for me. He would not subject me to this sort of arrangement and would be someone who understood me.

As time went by, people continued passing comments, 'You are too choosy, too modern. Your economic freedom has gone to your head.'

But my grandmother always supported me. She said, 'Don't talk to her like that. When the right man comes, she will agree.'

Then one day, one of my fathers' friends had his housewarming ceremony in Miraj (a prominent place in Maharashtra). As my father couldn't go, he said, 'Nali, there is a direct train in the morning. Attend the event and come back the next day. Anyway, you have college holidays.'

I was happy to get out of these marriage-related talks and comments and agreed.

The next day, I took the Kittur Chanamma Express, which reaches Miraj in the afternoon. As I am fond of food, I packed the ugly aluminium lunch box with upma, chutney powder, yogurt and a few fruits. I also bought a magazine. I got into the reserved compartment.

Most people get down at Hubli, leaving the compartment empty. Just when the train was about to leave, a young handsome man entered. I saw two old people on the platform, most likely his parents. They advised him after he sat as if sending a teenage girl out of the house for the first time, 'Be careful. Tell Anant I could not come because of old age. It is difficult for me. Don't come immediately after the function. Come the next day. Be careful and protect your wallet.'

The young man kept nodding through it all.

Though I was pretending to read, I was listening to every word. I could sense he was feeling embarrassed, seeing I had no parents around. He said shyly, 'Uncle, please go home. I will manage.'

I laughed in my head. 'What is there to manage for a six-hour train journey? What kind of a man is he?'

Though I wanted to speak to him, it did not feel right as he was young. I was worried about what he would think of me. If it were anybody else, I would have spoken and within a few stations, I would have known the person's history.

When the train reached Alnavar station, I opened my lunch box. He also opened his.

Finally, he spoke.

'Where are you going?' he asked.

That was enough for me to respond in a battery-operated doll-like way. 'I am going up to Miraj. And you?'

'I am going there, too.'

He paused for a minute and said, 'My name is Narasimha.'

I regretted the parents' choice of name. What a handsome man! For him, neither a human being nor a lion sort of name. It is an in-between, aggressive-sounding name and didn't suit him at all.

'Do you want to eat some besan ladoo?' he asked. 'Please have some.'

Before I could answer, he took the box and offered it to me. When I saw the box, I got the shock of my life. Not because of the ladoo, but because of the lunch box. It was a shiny steel box with NK engraved on the lid of the side. I just knew it was mine! But how could I ask this unknown young man to give it back to me and claim it as mine without proper evidence?

Instead of taking the laddoo, I said, 'Oh, your lunch box is very nice and shiny. Where did you buy it?'

Just then, the train whistle blew, and my words were drowned out.

He misheard and said, 'The ladoos? My aunt has made them. She is fond of me.'

Soon, we moved on to other topics and as usual, the train was late.

By the time we got down at Miraj, both of us were familiar with each other. But the unanswered question about the box remained with me. He had come for the same function, and he was working in the income tax department. Instead of one day, I stayed two days and so did he.

Anant kaka arranged visits for guests like us to Kolhapur, Kurundwad and surrounding places. We became quite friendly. I came to know his name was Narasimha Kulkarni (or NK too). The more I learnt, the more I realized that the boxes had certainly been exchanged.

When I reached home, my grandmother was happy. 'At last, you got a boy of your choice.'

'How?' I was taken aback.

'I heard you and Narasimha went around visiting places. How is the boy? I know his family. They are good. He is an orphan, raised by his uncle and aunt. Anant kaka gave me all the details and we are very happy.'

I had not realized that this was brewing against the backdrop of the wedding. Now I realized that Anant kaka and my father had planned to send me to Miraj to meet Narasimha.

I didn't have any objection. Neither did he.

But I wanted to be very clear about one thing—my lunch box.

I told my grandmother, 'I want to speak to him for five minutes before the marriage.'

What an unusual request for Hubli at the time! How bold I was! Uncertain, and in half a mind, our families agreed to a short meeting, saying that I should talk to him in the adjacent room to theirs so that they can keep an eye on us through the window.

I knew they also wanted to listen in to our conversation. Still, I agreed.

Narasimha came to my home with a smile. I was a little tensed, I was thinking of my precious lost lunch box all the time.

We exchanged awkward greetings.

My first question was, 'Where did you buy the lunch box?'

'Which one?'

I reminded him, 'The one you brought on the way to Miraj.'

'Oh that! Bhaskar is a friend. I went to his wedding but had to rush owing to a meeting. My aunt thought that I should at least eat something, so she took my box, and later brought it home. When we opened it, we were surprised to see a shiny new steel box had replaced my old aluminium one. I went back to the hall to return it to the owner. Someone said, "Oh it belongs to Lunch Box Nalini." Since I didn't know who that was, I came back.'

I laughed. 'I got my lunch box back, and a bonus with it—a groom.'

Epilogue

I grew up in a small town with a different culture. People there believed in direct conversations and avoided multi-layered soft talk—they are direct but very affectionate. Many times, it may look like an impractical way of living, but then what is the correct way of living?

I met many characters while growing up. These people did not have a degree or great jobs. They neither enjoyed great social status nor won any laurels for their work. Nonetheless, these characters have left an indelible impression on my mind.

In this book, there are fourteen such unique characters. They have nothing in common. They are mutually exclusive but collectively exhaustive.

Characters like Bindu inspired a love for Kannada, cultivated in me a respect for my mother tongue and helped me love the history of North Karnataka. If you do not know your past, you do not know your future.

People like Hema, the woman Friday, taught me to be selfless by helping whoever is in need. One need not have money but a compassionate heart to be philanthropic.

From Parvati's husband Banabhatta, I learnt that one need not express his or her love only through words but emotions prevail even in quietude.

Jeevaraj, the great miser of our town, became a great philanthropist by introspecting on his life when he fell sick. 'Going through your inner journey and learning from your experience is a better teacher than any guru,' was his message.

I am sure many people must have come across such people in their life but might not have recognized them. By reading this book, I am sure they can recollect, recognize, reward and applaud such simple people.

I bow down to my land—the land between the Krishna and Tungabhadra rivers—which was once upon a time, for many years, the capital of Karnataka. It has taught me many things that I cannot measure by titles, honours or money.

May my tribe increase.